With Best Wishes

Carol M Creasey

GW00601875

CANDIDLY CAROL

Also by Carol M. Creasey:

Biography:
My Life is Worth Living!

Fiction:
Fatal Obsession
Not Just an Affair
Evil Woman
Evil Woman...Takes Revenge
The Power of Love
One Moment of Madness

Candidly Carol

~ My Story ~

CAROL M. CREASEY

UNITED WRITERS
Cornwall

UNITED WRITERS PUBLICATIONS LTD
Ailsa, Castle Gate, Penzance, Cornwall.
www.unitedwriters.co.uk

British Library Cataloguing in Publication Data:
A catalogue record for this book is
available from the British Library.

ISBN 9781852001933

Printed and bound in Great Britain by
United Writers Publications Ltd.,
Cornwall.

I dedicate this to everyone who has
been a part of my life.
My husband, my children,
grandchildren, great-grandchildren,
my parents, stepmum and brother,
Keith and all my friends.
May God bless you all.

Chapter One

I was born in April 1944. My mother was able to give birth to me at home, and we lived in a semi-detached house in Coney Hall. For those who may not know where that is, it's a small town, on the outskirts of West Wickham, which is in the county of Kent.

Coney Hall was a great place to grow up in, as it was mostly common area, with parks, woods, just one high street with a few shops, and a very pretty local church. My parents lived on an estate which was newly built in 1944. Every road was named after the trees that were planted along the street. Our road was called Lime Tree Walk. In springtime, the whole area looked very beautiful with pink and white blossom on the trees everywhere, and at the top of our road were the local woods, with carpets of daffodils in April, closely followed by bluebells in May.

My father was a fireman, and during the war he risked his life many times to save people from burning houses when the bombs dropped. Shortly after I was born, my mother, brother and myself were evacuated to Leeds, where it was considered safer for us to be. We stayed there until the war finished, and when we returned home, my dad was waiting at the train station to meet us. When my mum put me into his arms, she said for the first time I cried. Apparently that was unusual for me as I was a happy baby, but I had no idea who this man was. However, it didn't take me long to bond with him, and I was always very proud of my amazing father.

Dad was quite short, about 5ft 7ins, not that it prevented him from being a fireman, it was his skill and endurance that mattered. He had brown hair, which became grey as he grew older, and blue eyes. During his life he took on many things, not being a man to sit down for long. When he came out of the fire service he set up his own business; and becoming a master builder he then formed his own company, hiring staff and building houses. In later years he campaigned to become a local political party leader. He also worked at the Royal Albert Hall as an usher; he didn't get paid for this, but he loved to see all the performances held there. He always looked so smart in his suit and tie, a handkerchief peeping out of his top jacket pocket; and his shoes shone, although Mum might have done that, and the crispness of his shirt would have been down to her too, as I never saw Dad with an iron in his hand. Mum was always the driving force behind him, the practical one. My dad was a great character, a little eccentric in his ways, but that is what I always loved about him. He also worked at Barkers in Kensington, and met quite a few celebrities when they were buying shoes, Frankie Howard being one of them. He adored my mother, he put her on a pedestal, and seeing how much he cared about her, and us, always made me feel very safe and loved.

My mother was a woman of very strong character, which I admired tremendously. She had to be the tough one because my dad would have spoiled me; he was Mr nice guy, even tempered, and, I think, anything for a quiet life. But mum wasn't having that. I don't actually ever remember her caning me, but as was normal in those days, she threatened to. Both my parents had suffered because my sister Shirley died before I was born. She was only two years old, and a frail little girl who suffered from asthma attacks. A neighbour was having fireworks on bonfire night, and invited my mum to take her. Whilst they were there, a jumping cracker went off and landed near to them, which set off a bad attack, and Shirley was hospitalised and put in an oxygen tent. After about a week in hospital she was fit to come home, but sadly for my mum, after my dad had left for work one morning, she went in to awaken Shirley and found she had died. Being a mother myself, I cannot possibly imagine what she went through, to find her baby had passed away, and then to have to call my dad back from work and having to tell him such news; she needed him to help her cope with it. Years after, if it was ever mentioned, she always had tears in her eyes, nobody had counselling in those days, you just had to get on with whatever life threw at you, but I don't think my mum ever stopped grieving.

As if that wasn't enough, after Shirley, my mum became pregnant again, and gave birth to a very big boy they named John, who was 10lbs in weight, but he only lived for six days, and appeared to be paralysed from the waist downwards. My mother was quite tiny, 5ft 2ins in height, with always a slim build, and she had to have forceps for the delivery, so was always convinced the forceps had harmed her baby. I am sure that if both of those children had been born now, they would have had a greater life expectancy. But it was very sad for both of my parents to lose their first two children.

My brother was born when my mum was twenty-seven. He was a slow developer, and he didn't walk until he was three years old, which was in 1940. Doctors told my mum he was 'backward', not a term we would use now, but in those days society was not sympathetic to anyone who was different. The doctor also told her not to push him too much, saying that if she did, 'It would drive any bit of sense that he had out of him.' The result of that was my parents in their efforts to do the right thing never expected too much of him.

Over the years, my brother Ron has coped in his own way. He went to a normal school, as then there was no other choice, he got teased and bullied because he was different, his cap was thrown down the road so many times on the way home, but he endured it all, and grew up knowing that some people in life are just not very nice.

He was a nice looking boy with blond curly hair, and very blue eyes, which always showed anxiety. Everything he attempted scared him, and I grew up knowing that my brother, although seven years older than me, was 'slow'. It grieved me to see other people taking advantage and ridiculing him, and I defended him, trying to make people realise that 'There by the grace of God go I.' Thank goodness that these days society is much kinder to vulnerable people like Ron.

He is going to be eighty-two this year, and with a little support from us he leads a normal life. He still drives his car, and he lives in sheltered housing. Since he has been there he has learned to cook, and he manages his money very well. I am very proud of him. Although everything in life has been much harder for him,

9

he can lead a normal life. When he was at school, he tried very hard, and a kindly teacher, in recognition of this, made sure he always got an award for being the most hard working boy.

Now having read all this, you might think my parents were not happy people, but believe me they were. They were both strong minded and coped amazingly with the traumas I have described, realising that life is for living, and what doesn't break you makes you stronger. They both had a great sense of humour; which was just as well, because after having my brother, who was an obedient child, then I came along, feisty, independent and strong minded. My dad was very proud of that, and said I should have been a boy. I was always in shorts and climbing trees; in fact, I have always got on better with men than women, I find them less complicated, and more honest and straightforward.

Having said that, I have some very dear girlfriends, who have been very loyal to me over the years, and they know who they are. I have to add that although I was quite loud in the classroom, and always in trouble for talking too much, I have grown up to be quite the opposite: I am shy, and I have to really get to know people before I tell them much about my life. I am always the one who is standing listening at a party, and part of me envies people who appear to be the life and soul; they have so much self esteem and confidence. I would love to be like them. I think the good thing about being an author is that I can put my feelings and emotions into written words within a book.

I have tried to remember back to when I was very young. I have a memory of a cold night in winter and my mother dressing me in a very warm coat, and I was wearing a pink fluffy bonnet. It was very foggy, and I also had a scarf wound round my mouth so that the fog couldn't make me cough. I was about three years old at that time. Ron always worried about me, he said I must hold Mum's hand. I think some of my daring caused him worry, he never liked it when I climbed trees, he was convinced I would fall down. On this occasion I did hold her hand, and he was the other side of her.

I always accepted that Ron needed more of my parents' attention than I did, and I never felt any jealousy or sibling rivalry. I can honestly say that I liked my feeling of independence. Even at three years, there was an incident when a bus came along and we went to get onto it. The bus conductor, seeing my mother with two children, and me being just a tot, sprang down from the platform and picked me up, saying, "Let me help your little girl, this step is far too high for her." Mum was about to thank him, but to her horror, as soon as he let go of me, I jumped back off the step and got up on my own. She said that even at three years old, it was clear to see I already had a mind of my own.

I can remember back to when I was four years old, hearing on the radio that our Princess (as she was then) Elizabeth had been safely delivered of a son, Prince Charles; the date was 14th November 1948. Because I was only four years old, I believed that the postman had brought him, as that was the only sort of delivery that I understood!

The first school I went to was an annexe of Gates Green Road School at Coney Hall. These days it's now a block of flats, but back in 1949, you went there to begin with, and then moved to the next school within a year or so. I can remember that first day so clearly. In spite of all my bravado, I didn't want to let go of my mother's hand; the playground looked huge. Of course it wasn't, but I was looking with the eyes of a five year old.

I had never attended a nursery or playschool. My mum didn't go to work, my dad being the sole provider, as it so often was then. So all of a sudden I was cut off from Mum's apron strings, and put in a class amongst about thirty other boys and girls of the same age. I was immediately aware the boys were much more fun; they larked around and ran about at playtime, whereas the girls spent most of playtime doing cat's cradle with bits of wool, or styling each other's hair. There was absolutely nothing feminine about me then. I always loved sports, and there were other girls like me, so we tended to move in the same friendship circles, playing hopscotch and skipping.

On that first day we were given some simple sums to do. I felt quite confident that I knew the answers, but then the teacher said, "Add your initials to the paper afterwards." I didn't know what she was talking about, what on earth were initials? I suppose, at five years old, I should have known. There was a boy sitting near to me, his name was Graham Cooke, and I had already discovered he was quite a laugh. I whispered to him in desperation. "What are initials?"

He stopped flicking his pencil, and grinned.

"If you tell me the answers to the questions, I will tell you."

I didn't hesitate, or even think about morals, it was my first day at school, so I wrote the answers down and slipped the piece of paper to him. A reply came back very shortly.

"Your name is Carol Maureen Edwards, so your initials are C M E."

I then realised how stupid I had been not to know; I had been too engrossed in getting my sums right. I think that was probably one time that Graham got all his sums right, and whether our teacher guessed he had a bit of help, I have no idea, but I didn't suffer any conscience about it.

I always used to wake up early in the morning. My mum said I was always on the go until I went to bed. I can remember sunny days, there seemed to be many of them; light mornings, and the clink of milk bottles as the milkman did his round. He was a very cheerful man, and he whistled. Sometimes my mum would be putting out the washed out milk bottles just in time for him to collect.

I moved into the bigger school which was situated in Gates Green Road when I was about seven. From where we lived, there was only one road to cross, which was never that busy, and then a walk down an alleyway, which had houses either side of it, and you turned right, and the school was about two hundred yards along. I felt at seven that I wanted to walk to school on my own; I didn't need Mum any more. Most families had only one car, which the father took to work, and the mothers walked the children to school, or got the bus. My mother never learned to drive, if my dad wasn't around she travelled on trains or buses. I can remember her words: "As long as you behave yourself." That was her stock phrase for me, because I did things that Ron never even dreamed off. She was always telling me to walk on the pavement, and not to balance on people's walls and walk along them. On more than one occasion, there had been a rap on the window telling me to get down.

I was so determined to be independent that I stopped jumping on the walls, and walked to school with my friends. I had realised by then what I liked at school. Any activity that was sport was fun, and I was really good at spelling, so I enjoyed English lessons, and writing compositions was also fun. Being able to create characters and stories has always been enjoyable for me. I didn't like maths, although I could add up quite quickly, I couldn't see why I needed to do logarithms and all the fancy stuff, and I also found sciences boring. Although I did love Nature; going for walks and collecting flowers to press, I found fun.

In 1950, Dad re-concreted the patio of our garden and made me a swing. It was simply a flat piece of wood, with strong twine to support it, but I loved it. He carved his initials and 1950 into the concrete, as he said it would go down in history. He also made me a sledge, and when we took it out in the snow, he used it more than I did. He hurtled down a hill on the common, and I was running behind yelling that it was my turn. All my friends thought I had an amazing dad, so the swing and the sledge were very well used.

On 15th August 1950 Princess Anne was born. I have always been very much a royalist, just as my parents were, and because I was so young when they were born, I feel as if I grew up with Charles and Anne. They didn't get the sort of press coverage that the Royal Family all get now, but I remember that every time I saw a photograph of Anne, she had beautiful white blonde hair, and it was very curly.

My parents were accomplished ballroom dancers. My dad had, in fact, taught dancing at one time; he had also become a member of the Masons. They went to lots of balls, and I loved watching my mother getting ready. She had always been slim and small boned, but she wore a heavy corset that she had to lace up at the front, because she said it would be unthinkable to display a bulging stomach. She said that after four babies, her muscles were gone. When I saw her without her corset, she had the tiniest of tummies, in no way offensive, but she had been brought up to think she must conceal any bulges. I know that many women in the past did the same thing, they suffered in the name of fashion, even squashing their feet into shoes that were too small for them; Mum didn't do that. But one of her friends did, and when she became middle aged, she suffered bunions and all sorts of feet problems, and regularly had to visit the chiropodist.

Mum wore beautiful dresses with swirling underskirts, her hair was piled on top of her head and she always smelt wonderful. She didn't wear heavy make-up, she didn't need to, she had a small elfin face, with a turned up nose, and was often likened to the actress Jane Wyman, who was very popular at that time. Dad always looked smart in his suits and shiny shoes; to me they were the most handsome couple.

13

At the age of seven in 1951, I was devastated when my mum told me we were going to move to Shirley. My parents had found a bigger house, my dad's business was thriving, and they wanted to better themselves. I didn't want to leave all my friends, or the freedom that I enjoyed at Coney Hall. I didn't want to go to a new school either, Gates Green Road School was a great one. I always got a good report from the teachers, and I was happy there.

But contracts had been signed and exchanged, and my parents promised me I would like my new life. I trusted them, but always carried a wealth of happy memories inside me of Coney Hall, my first home.

Shirley was a small town just outside Croydon, in Surrey. It had a high street with local shops, a library, a recreation ground, and woods, as well as Shirley Hills, a local beauty spot, which many people visited. Our house was bigger, but still semi-detached. The rooms were big. We had a garage, a breakfast room as well as a kitchen, and a very large garden. There was a paved area outside the lounge with a sun dial. The lounge was kept as a 'best' room, it had velvet curtains and a thick fitted carpet. I lived there for twelve years until I was married, but I had left my heart in Coney Hall.

Not long after moving my mum and dad took us on a holiday to the Isle of Wight. It was a holiday camp, and they held fancy dress competitions. My mum made me amazing costumes out of crepe paper, so I entered first as Goldilocks; my long blonde hair was worn loose on this occasion, and I held a bowl and spoon in my hand. The second time I was red riding hood, with a cloak made entirely of crepe paper, it even covered my head. On both occasions I won first prize.

Later that week, we went out for a walk. I was running about, but both my mother and Ron were nervous about the cliff edge. My dear dad, in an effort to keep me safe, picked me up to give me a piggy back, but then he slipped and fell back on me with all his weight. I will never forget the pain this caused me, and how upset my dad was. He carried me in his arms to the local doctor, and mum was doing her best to stop me from screaming, as I sounded like I was being murdered. The doctor's surgery was a very old house with low ceilings, and as we entered, my dad in his agitation turned suddenly and I hit my head on the low ceiling, and immediately started howling again!

My leg was broken and I had to have it plastered up, so this put pay to my activities. I had to sit with my leg supported for the rest of the holiday, and that really cramped my style, and taught me a lesson not to go near cliff edges again.

At Shirley the local church was called St John's Church, and right next to it was my next school, St John's School. I was happy enough there. When I was eight our class was invited to dance round the maypole on the Vicar's lawn. As soon as I saw the beautiful blue taffeta dress I was going to wear, I temporarily forgot I was a tomboy. All our parents were sitting there proudly watching us and drinking tea as we danced round the maypole. It was a beautiful summer's day without any hint of rain or dark skies.

During that year, which was 1952, one day at school we were called into a special assembly, and told that our king, George VI, had died. Everyone was very sad, he had been ill with throat cancer, and was in his fifties, which at the time seemed old to me, but of course it wasn't.

At the age of nine, I discovered, when I climbed our garden fence, there was waste ground outside some tennis courts, so we often used to hang out there. We lit bonfires, and generally made nuisances of ourselves, and had to bunk quickly over the fence if anyone arrived to play tennis. On one day when I was climbing back, I got a splinter in my finger, but didn't worry too much about it, and didn't mention it to my mum. Within a couple of days I had blood poisoning, and was admitted to Waddon Hospital, as I also had scarlet fever, which in the 1950s, could be very dangerous. Luckily I made a good recovery after a couple of weeks, and returned to school. When my mum found out how I got the splinter, I was forbidden to go over that fence again.

Later that year, which was 1953, our new Queen Elizabeth II was crowned. She was very beautiful, and was married to Prince Philip of Greece, who was known as The Duke of Edinburgh.

Dad's building business was going well, so he bought a piece of land on a bungalow estate at Herne Bay. It was somewhere we had already visited and liked. First of all he put a caravan on the land until he received planning permission, then a bungalow was built so we could spend holidays there. We went as often as we could. The only problem was, I was car sick, and the journey took over two hours, as it was before the motorways were built, and we had to pass through the busy city of Sittingbourne. My dad tried everything to stop my car sickness, and my mum bought me some pills called 'Quells', but nothing worked until I grew out of it years later.

When I was eleven, I took my eleven-plus examination. I didn't think I had done that well. One of the papers was a space test, and I ran out of time and didn't finish it. But when the results came through I had passed, and would be going to a local grammar school. Mum and Dad were thrilled, and I was rewarded with a new bike. Mum praised me quietly; I knew she didn't want to make Ron feel bad because life was a struggle for him, and I understood. We went to look over Archbishop Tenison's, it was a very old and dark building, but we didn't mind, as they were building a new up to date school in Selborne Road in Croydon, which would have airy classrooms, and lots of sports facilities, which I liked the sound of. So I started at the old building for a year, knowing there were better things to come, and my mum went out and bought me my smart royal blue uniform from the school shop, which she said cost a fortune and I was to look after it. Little did I know, when I started at my grammar school, just how much my life would change.

I only had one grandparent left when I was born, my mother's mother. She lived over at Barkingside, in just a couple of rooms, and I remember her coming to stay, and taking me out to buy sweets. She died in 1955, when I was eleven, and she was in her seventies. Mum shed tears, and so did I, because I missed my Nana, we had a special relationship.

Chapter Two

I had found school work relatively easy at my primary school, but at grammar school it was completely different. Instead of always being near the top of the class in English, I was only about midway. There were children there far brainier than me. I could not have been an easy pupil to teach. I found maths and sciences boring, as well as history and geography. To make it worse, the teachers we had for those subjects did not inspire me in any way; in my eyes they were old and boring, and we all had pet names for them which fitted their characters. When you are eleven, someone of thirty seems old.

I always enjoyed English and spelling, and I found I had a flair for languages; French and Latin became part of my curriculum. Our French teacher was such a nice man, his name was Mr Davis, and he spoke about life in France, and all sorts of things that made learning more interesting. I was hoping to visit France, and we did, he led a school trip there, and we spent a very enjoyable week experiencing French food and attempting to speak to the locals in our garbled and very English accents.

The deputy headmistress took us for Latin. She was strict, her grey hair was tied very tightly into a bun, she always wore a grey tweed suit, black lace-up shoes and no stockings or tights. I doubt her face had ever seen make-up; she was truly married to her job, and when she spoke, her mouth turned up on one side. To me she was exactly what the word spinster meant, and part of me felt sorry for her if she was alone. She must have been a good teacher as, because of her, I became very interested in Latin. Even though people sometimes say it is a dead language, that is not true, Latin can help with other languages, such as Spanish or Italian, and also English words are derived from Latin.

Just after I started at Tenison's School, I had my first crush. It would have made life easier if he was at that school, but Billy Douse was at the local secondary modern school, and he lived on a prefab estate, which was just a bike ride away from where I lived. I started to see boys, not as just mates, but exciting companions, and Billy had very dark hair and striking green eyes, he was a year older than me, and showed no interest in me whatsoever, which made him even more attractive to me. He rode a bike and he loved to show off, letting go with his hands, and other tricks that held me and a few other girls in awe. But when you are eleven, you are fickle, and a few months later, I could barely remember his name. I realised I was now reaching an age where the opposite sex were not just mates, they were mysterious interesting people.

Well this is how I felt, but boys at that age would rather die than be seen with a girl. Although our school was a co-educational school, the boys sat on one side of the room, then there was a gangway, and the girls sat on the other. Most of the desks were double, so pupils sat in pairs. If a boy misbehaved, his punishment was to be put next to a girl, and all his friends would tease him mercilessly about it afterwards.

As I mentioned earlier, I was a bit loud at school. I spoke too much, and didn't stop quickly enough when the teacher came in the room, so was usually yelled at, or made to come and stand at the front. I was a giggler, too ready to laugh at anything, and once I got a fit of the giggles, I found it very difficult to stop. When I read this I realise I must have been a teacher's worst nightmare. I remember when my biology teacher, who was only twenty-seven, and most of the girls adored (but not me), heard me giggling; he picked up a rubber and threw it across the room at me, it whistled across my ear and stung, having the desired effect of making me stop laughing. I could just imagine the horror if a teacher did that today; life has changed so much.

My best friend at school was a girl called Paula Revell; she was much quieter than me. I had several good friends; there was Lilian, Margaret, Pat, and Geraldine, but sadly, after we left school, went to work and got married, we gradually lost touch.

18

Paula went to live in Australia, but I have no idea about the others.

I had also made friends with girls around where I lived in Shirley. One particular close friend was Sylvia Freeman, she was a year younger than me, and went to Shirley Secondary Modern School, which was up near to the primary school I had attended. Sylvia was very pretty and her hair always looked lovely, so I was not surprised that she left school at fifteen and became an apprentice at our local hairdressers. We used to take it in turns to spend our evenings together at each other's houses. We usually got together about once a week. Sylvia was very much into nice hairstyles and make-up, whereas I was more active; at school I was in the netball, rounders and hockey teams. Games was my favourite time at school, but even with our different personalities, we had a close friendship for many years.

At the age of eleven, I competed in the Kent championships. I was a sprinter and I made it into the final. But I did even better as part of the relay team, as we came second. All these years later, I still have the medal, and I remember feeling so proud when we were all presented with them.

In 1958, when I was fourteen, one of my friends came up with an idea of 'Rock and Roll Afternoons'. Some of the girls were beginning to like the boys in our class, and the plan was to take it in turns to hold these events at each other's houses, to keep it casual, and invite the boys along too. They then wanted to dress up and wear make-up, anything to get themselves noticed by the boys. I was mad about Elvis at the time, and other friends were into Cliff, so we made sure we had plenty of their records to play.

None of the boys in my class appealed to me at all. Some of them had spots, but love is blind, and Geraldine and Paula could see past the spots. But I didn't want to be a party pooper, so on these afternoons, I swapped my shorts for a full skirt, which was enhanced by a whalebone petticoat; such was the fashion at the time. I had spent ages threading the bone through the top of the frill, so when I walked the skirt swung about, which was great when I was jiving, but when I look back now I realise I must have looked like a walking lampshade. All my friends were similarly dressed. We thought we were really cool, and I remember that when we sat down on a chair, it was hard to keep our skirts under control as the whalebone caused them to spring up.

19

None of the girls really managed to snare a boy at that time. What happened was the girls spent most of the afternoon on their feet, jiving with each other and hoping the boys would notice them, and the boys didn't dance, they just came along for the free food that was laid out, and if they could smuggle any sort of drink in to liven up the proceedings they did. These Saturday afternoon events lasted for about a year, until one day a boy brought some cider. All the girls, including me, got a bit merry, and we were all rolling about laughing, then someone was sick on the sofa (not me) and Geraldine's parents arrived home unexpectedly; we all got slung out, and she was forbidden to go to any more of the events. Geraldine's mum knew my mum, so she regaled her with the details. It hadn't been my turn yet to invite everyone to my house, and after that I never got the opportunity, and nobody else did either. I even tried in desperation to ask my dad 'If I could have a few friends round for a rock and roll afternoon?' believing daddy could never deny me anything. His reply was:

"If it's OK with your mother." But, of course, it wasn't; and I have to say that over the years, when I wanted to do something, instead of asking Mum first, I tried my luck on Dad, but he was always loyal to Mum and supported whatever decisions she made. And looking back I now know that she was absolutely right. She only wanted me to grow up safely and respect people, and have the right values. I am glad she was strict.

During that year of 1958 my brother bought a motorbike and passed his test. I often used to ride pillion on it, and he joined a club, so we used to go out with them all on a Sunday afternoon. One particular day he went over a bump in the road, which dislodged my foot and I caught my heel in the spokes of the bike, and a piece of my heel was literally hanging off. Mum and Dad took me to Croydon General Hospital, and they mopped up all the blood, and stitched my skin back. I was none the worse for wear afterwards, although the white scar of the stitches remained. My brother was mortified about what had happened, although it was not his fault, just an unforeseen accident. But soon after that he got rid of his motorbike and bought a Lambretta. He felt that as it had a platform to rest my feet, it would be safer, and it was.

When I was fifteen years old and Sylvia was fourteen, we were out for a walk at Shirley Hills one day. We had taken Jasper, my wire haired fox terrier with us. During my childhood we had dogs; my parents both loved them, and Ron and I grew up to feel the same way.

Suddenly a big German Shepherd bounded over, and I held my breath, as Jasper was only a small dog, but very friendly. I needn't have worried, not only was he friendly, but also his owner came over quickly to get him. When I saw this boy standing there, a feeling which I didn't understand at the time, coursed through my insides. He was tall and slim, his brown eyes were limpid, his skin slightly olive, and his hair was dark brown. He had tried to tame it with Brylcreem, but a stray curl flopped over his forehead. His handsome face quite took my breath away; he was like a film star, and he knew it. Sylvia had noticed him too, and her face broke out into a bright smile.

"I do apologise for Rupert, but he's just a big softie."

He addressed me, but before I could say anything, Sylvia spoke up.

"Jasper is friendly too, isn't he Carol?"

I gulped, conscious of the fact that I was dressed like a boy in shorts, my hair was untidy, and I didn't look the slightest bit feminine. This boy was making me feel that I didn't want to be a tomboy any more, I wanted to be more like Sylvia. Her hair was neat, and she had a summer skirt and blouse on.

He introduced himself as Howard Richards. I was so under his spell that I saw his lips moving, but didn't really hear the words. It was like meeting a famous celebrity, and I was struck dumb. Not so Sylvia, she was right upfront, chatting away to him, and telling him our names. He introduced his companion as John. I had been so mesmerised by Howard, I hadn't even noticed John, and when I did look at him, it wasn't for long. He was short and stocky, a round face and solid build. His face was kindly, but he just didn't have the allure that positively shone out of Howard.

Howard invited us to go to his house, he said his parents were cool about him bringing friends home, and he didn't seem to mind that we were also bringing Jasper with us. I was watching him as we all walked together towards his house, which was very near to Shirley Hills. I was watching Sylvia through his eyes; at only fourteen, she looked older. She wore make-up, the fashion at the moment was what I called 'slit eyes', which meant that oriental looking eyes were achieved by painting the corners with eye liner, and Sylvia had done it beautifully, making her eyes really noticeable. Her hair as usual was impeccably groomed, whereas I had the tousled look, no make-up, and my old shorts on, because I had been rolling on the ground playing with Jasper. So to me it was obvious who he would like, and I felt so miserable, because the effect he was having on me was mind-blowing. I wished I wasn't so boyish; I hated being thin, the boys at school ragged me all the time about it, singing *Bony Maronie*, a popular song at the time, as I walked past them.

When we arrived at his house, in a private road, we were both taken aback. It was set in its own grounds, with lots of trees around, and a long drive leading up to the house, which stood resplendent, the sun shining on it. The gardens both front and back were beautifully kept, and there was a man working in the garden as we approached, which I imagined was the gardener, but in fact turned out to be Howard's father. He barely raised an eyebrow as we passed, and as we went through the front door, the voice of Howard's mother floated down the stairs.

"If you want some lunch Howard it's in the fridge."

"Later Mum, I've brought some friends back."

At these words his mother appeared, a kindly lady, she was dressed in a skirt and blouse, her hair was permed, and she looked a bit distracted as she absent-mindedly ran her fingers through it.

Howard introduced us, and explained we were going to the den to play records.

"I'll bring you down some cold drinks and some snacks then?" she suggested, smiling warmly.

I took an instant liking to her, she seemed a little scatty; one glance around showed a beautiful house, but it was very untidy and disorganised.

"I put some towels down somewhere," she said glancing around, then she spotted something underneath a newspaper, and pounced triumphantly. "Here they are."

The den turned out to be a large room down a flight of stairs separate from the rest of the house. It had a fitted carpet, burgundy coloured, there were books ranged all around the shelves, a TV and a record player. There was also a jukebox, just like the ones I had seen in the coffee bars in Croydon. Sylvia and I were both very in awe of the set up.

Howard was clearly enjoying showing off his home, and I was enjoying being there, and with parents who were more than willing for him to bring home a couple of girls and an extra dog, how great was that. Admittedly both Sylvia and I lived in much smaller houses, but usually we asked our parents in advance if we could bring friends home, in comparison this seemed a very easy-going lifestyle.

We spent a memorable afternoon playing Elvis and Cliff records, as well as Little Richard and Fats Domino. Sylvia and I had a jive, Howard and John stood by. John didn't say much, he seemed to be in Howard's shadow, and once or twice I caught Howard looking at me, and I guessed he was comparing me to my glamorous best friend. Later in the afternoon they seemed to be whispering at the other end of the room, so my fears seemed to be confirmed, I had fallen in love with a boy who was about to be my best friend's boyfriend.

When we finally left to go home, we had arranged to meet them in the same place on Sunday, and I was already deciding that it would be my last time. I had fallen hard for him. It was a completely new experience for me, and I knew I could not bear to see him with Sylvia. I had to forget him, I wasn't even looking for a boyfriend; I was only fifteen and until now boys had just been mates to me.

"Well you certainly made a hit with Howard!" remarked Sylvia, as we walked home. Her face looked very disappointed.

"What! He was whispering with you."

"Yes, asking me to put in a good word for him. He seems very full of himself, but as far as you are concerned, he doesn't know if you like him."

"Like him?" I echoed. Nothing made sense to me any more. I couldn't believe that, with his film star looks (in fact when I thought about it, he did resemble a slightly younger Elvis), he would look at me.

"Yes, you seemed very casual towards him, like a mate. The way you are with all boys. I liked him too, but you are my friend, and it's you he's interested in."

Those words thrilled me so much, but I also felt sorry for Sylvia. She had fallen for him too, and sometimes love hurts. I vowed to make more of myself at that moment, and to be more feminine.

*   *   *   *

23

By the time 1960 came around, our Queen, after a period of ten years, gave birth to another child. Prince Andrew was born on 19th February 1960.

My romance with Howard lasted for a year until I was sixteen. Every time I looked at him I felt so proud, and I always viewed him through rose-coloured glasses. Sylvia paired up with John, and we went out together at the weekends. We usually went to the pictures on Saturday afternoon, and then onto the coffee bar afterwards to play the jukebox. My favourite song at that time was *A fool such as I* by Elvis. I grew my hair long, and made the most of my twenty-two inch waist by wearing skirts with a blouse tucked inside with a black elasticated belt. I have never worn heavy make-up, and with my fair skin, slit eyes would have looked ridiculous, but a little eye shadow and mascara, and some lipstick, gave me a bit of colour. Because of Howard I left my tomboy ways behind.

He charmed his way into my mother's good books, and I could tell my dad was a bit jealous of him. Our parents made friends with each other, and they went to visit each other sometimes and play cards. Howard met me every day after school. He went to a private school, but he used to get the bus to my school, and then we would walk home over Shirley Hills holding hands.

He was the first true love of my life, and during that year together I floated along in a dream, scarcely able to believe my luck. It was a very innocent relationship; it felt very pure, even though I had very strong feelings for him.

Just after my sixteenth birthday, in April 1960, my whole world felt like it had collapsed when he told me it was over. I didn't want to believe it; my dream had gone, and it was only a dream, because he had another girlfriend. Her name was Simone, and weirdly he asked me if he could bring her to meet me, he insisted he wanted us to still be friends.

I didn't want him to see how heartbroken I felt, so I agreed. Of course, I hated her on sight, but put on an 'I don't care' attitude. None of this helped me at school; I couldn't concentrate on anything, not homework or revision. So when I took my GCEs, as they were called in those days, I failed all my English papers, and only passed French and Latin. I really had let my parents down, but there were no recriminations. I almost wished they had bawled me out, because my emotions were all over the place. All my years at a grammar school had been wasted because I had loved and lost at the most important time in my school life.

b

Chapter Three

I had already been interviewed by the careers officer before I took my exams. Because of my interest in Latin and French, a job in a travel agency seemed a good idea. I could have travelled up to London and earned quite a good wage. Booking clerks were always needed, and I knew enough French to hold a conversation if we should get someone wanting to book who didn't speak English.

There was a vacancy at Grants Travel Bureau in Croydon, which was just a bus ride away. I went for the interview and was offered the job, then mum stepped in.

She explained that at work I must look the part and be smart. So we went shopping and bought a black and white check suit; the jacket had black buttons, and I wore it with a white blouse for relief, and it had two skirts to alternate, one was a pencil skirt, the other was pleated. At sixteen I was very immature, and respected my mother's guidance, but that suit became like a school uniform which I was happy to change out of as soon as I got home.

Just before I started my job, Paula and I decided we would like to spend a holiday together, as we had left school and would soon go our separate ways. Our parents were not impressed, pointing out we were only just sixteen, and being young girls we needed to be protected. My mum saved the day when she suggested we go to Margate. Friends of theirs had a bed and breakfast there; they also had two teenage sons. I had known Alan and Brian when we lived at Coney Hall, but that was some ten years ago. The idea was the boys could accompany us, and their parents could keep a check on what time we got home in the evening. I was quite disappointed when I saw the boys; they were at a gawky age, and compared to Howard, they just didn't cut it. Nevertheless we had a nice week with good weather, and I came home refreshed and ready to start my new job.

It didn't take me long to get settled into my job, and as our bureau was situated within a department store, I soon made new friends. I got paid a 'training wage', as they called it, of four guineas, and during my time there it hardly increased at all. Out of that I gave my mum two pounds for my keep; the rest went towards clothes, shoes and fares to work, and there was never much left. Jenny was a typist in the offices above the store, she wore smart pencil skirts and high heels, and her auburn brown hair was naturally curly, although she was always trying to straighten it. Jean also worked there; she was a vivacious Anglo Indian girl with beautiful dark hair and brown eyes.

Those two were my closest friends. I was very touched when, after admiring a white pleated skirt in a shop one day, Jenny told me she had won some money, and insisted on taking me there and buying it for me, as well as a pale blue top to go with it.

I used to go out dancing twice a week to the Orchid Ballroom at Purley; Wednesday evening and Saturday evening. It wasn't ballroom dancing, I had not inherited my parents' skills. This venue used to host some of the biggest pop stars of the time, and our greatest thrill was to get up to the edge of the area with the bold lighting where they were performing. The stage rotated round. When I wasn't jiving with my friends, I was watching stars such as Johnny Kidd and the Pirates, Marty Wilde, Joe Brown, just to name a few, but we were never able to get close enough to meet them properly or get an autograph.

My social life was also spent in the coffee bars that had sprung up in Croydon at that time, playing the jukebox and chatting with my friends. Sunday was a day I usually spent at home. I used to lay in until late morning, when my mum would bring me up a cup of tea, then we had dinner, and I had a lazy afternoon. Sunday was my day off from work, and the shop closed for a half day on Wednesday as well.

The following summer, when I was seventeen, Jenny asked me if I wanted to go on holiday with her and her cousin to Torquay in Devon. I had not met her cousin, but felt sure we would get on.

It had taken me a year to get over my break-up from Howard, partly because he was still very much in my life. He had so many girlfriends, none of them lasted long, and he always brought them round to see if I approved. Our parents continued to be friends, and his mother often invited me up to afternoon tea; she seemed to be fond of me, but she didn't get involved in our break-up, or mention any of his new girlfriends.

One year later, I was still affected by his good looks and the way he smiled when he came in a room, but I no longer saw him through rose-tinted glasses. His charm always disarmed people. I no longer had that rush of jealousy when I met his latest girlfriend, and I no longer hoped he would come back to me.

Jenny remarked that this holiday would be an opportunity for me to meet someone new, although she already had a boyfriend at home. I wasn't that fussed, I was looking forward to enjoying warm sunny days on the beach and swimming in the sea.

Her cousin Gloria, Jenny and I all shared a big bedroom at the hotel. We had travelled by train, it took several hours, and the first impression of Gloria was that she liked to keep herself to herself. She was an ordinary looking girl with brown straight hair, and I assumed she was shy. But the next morning, when we got up to wash and dress for breakfast, I was amazed to see Gloria repeatedly getting dressed and undressed. In the end we went to breakfast ahead of her. Jenny explained that nobody would take her on holiday because she did this all the time. Looking back now with more knowledge, there was clearly a problem, other than her just being difficult, but at that time it was something that was completely new to me. Jenny was quite tough with her, and leaving her to come down later seemed to work, because by the end of the week, hunger had won, and Gloria sat with us at breakfast.

We spent our days on the beach. The sun was warm, the sky was blue, and the sea was inviting. Jenny and Gloria didn't get their costumes wet, they sunbathed, but I did. There were a couple of boys on holiday, and they chatted to them. One was particularly attracted to Jenny, so he became her holiday romance for that week. His friend was very tall and his name was Roger, he tried to pair himself with me, but I was not a bit interested, so I ended up spending most of my time with Gloria. She had no interest in boys, so boringly we stayed at the hotel in the evenings and watched television.

When we returned home, we went back to work, and after the holiday, felt a bit flat. Leaving work that Saturday evening, we were heading towards the coffee bar, when three young men could be seen walking on the other side of the road. One of them was extremely handsome, he looked very much like the DJ Tony Blackburn, with his dark hair and arresting looks. One of the girls suggested we pretend to be drunk and fall about, then they might come over and pick us up. Well it sounded like a laugh. I clung to a lamp post proclaiming my head was spinning, and it worked. The handsome one came gallantly over and supported me. My friend was not impressed as she had set her sights on him.

As it happened his name was Tony, but I was not attracted to him in spite of his good looks. We just became mates, and all went round to the coffee bar, where we admitted that we were not drunk. It's amazing what daft things you can get away with when you are a teenager, and those young men just laughed it off.

We met up with them again the next week, and Tony brought his friend with him. His name was Mick Bedford. Well that is how he introduced himself, but his parents always called him Michael. Mick was the opposite of Tony, he had blond tight curls, blue eyes, and he was in the Merchant Navy. He seemed very interesting, and I was immediately attracted to him. When we went home I was disappointed, as I had been hoping that he might ask for my phone number.

He was doing short trips between England and Belgium, and away for about four days at a time. When he returned he rang me up, he said he had checked first with Tony if we were a couple and Tony had given him my number. He asked if he could take me out, and I knew then that I was definitely over Howard.

Howard continued to keep in touch; I couldn't really do anything about it because sometimes he came round to see my mother. I did notice that the atmosphere between Howard and Mick was a bit frosty. Mick said he couldn't work out why he kept hanging around.

Then Howard came round one day with very sad news. His parents were divorcing, his mother had left the family home and was living in rented accommodation, and she had taken Rupert their dog with her. His younger brother Jeremy was staying at the house, and Howard himself said he wasn't sure where he was going, but he wanted to start a new life. Then to my surprise he asked me to get engaged and come with him.

A few months earlier and my heart would have lifted at those words, but now I was with Mick, and my crush on Howard was definitely fading. I let him down gently. I knew I would always have an affection for him, but I also knew we were not suited. He was a restless person and I doubted if he could ever truly settle down.

So he went out of my life, and my romance with Mick blossomed. My mother liked him very much, and thought we were well suited, but my dad didn't. Mum insisted he was always polite to him, and she told me that because in his eyes I was still his little girl, probably he wouldn't think any man was worthy of me.

My mum and dad never really argued much. My dad had always been happy to let my mum be the decision maker, so I was surprised and distressed to hear raised voices between them quite frequently. Then one morning I found my mother in tears in the kitchen, and she told me that my dad was going bankrupt and she had no idea what would happen to us? This really scared me. My dad had done his best to keep it from all of us, but it had reached a head; my dad was so desperate, that in a rare emotional moment, I heard him threaten to leave my mother if she didn't stop 'nagging him'.

But they say when the going gets tough, the tough get going, and that is what happened to us. My dad's best friend was a solicitor, and he was also a Mason, and Masons stick together in times of trouble. Virtually overnight the house was transferred into my mother's name so the debt collectors couldn't touch it. Back in 1961, houses were nearly always just in the man's name, a wrong which was put right when women also started to go to work to help pay the mortgage. The bungalow at Herne Bay also had to be sold, sadly.

Mum was fifty-one, and she hadn't worked since Ron was born. She had been a shorthand typist, having trained at Pitmans, but her confidence had gone. Nevertheless her determination to support my dad and get our lives back on track spurred her to go to a local restaurant and ask if they needed extra staff. She started off peeling vegetables in the kitchen, then she did the cooking when the chef left. She also did waitressing, and in the end the lady who owned it gave her the job of running the restaurant because she was opening another one. By that time she was earning a good wage.

Dad explained that he had built some houses for a local council but had never been paid. He had tried to get the money and hadn't succeeded, and he could not maintain the loss. It was a traumatic situation for a while as we couldn't answer the phone when people were ringing up to demand payment for various bills, including his own workers.

Nowadays bankruptcy means very little, the shame has gone, but in 1961, not only did it appear in our local paper, but also my mum had gone back to work in a kitchen, something she didn't share with many people, as she always worried about what other people thought.

Mum had a friend whose husband worked in County Hall in London, and because my dad had quite a few qualifications he was invited for an interview. He passed, and worked there as an architect and surveyor until they retired him at sixty-five.

I shared our precarious predicament with Mick, which made us become closer, and after a year together, we got engaged when I was eighteen. We didn't want a long engagement, and we were saving up to put a deposit on a house, so I left the travel bureau and joined a company that supplied background music in shops, hotels etc, something that was just becoming popular. I stayed there for a year, and then I saw a job advertised in an insurance company as a motor insurance clerk. They were asking for someone with GCE in Maths, which I didn't have, but I tried to put on my best side at the interview, telling them how much I enjoyed studying French and Latin at school. My interviewer seemed to like me, so I got the job. My wage went up to the dizzy heights of ten pounds per week, which meant I could save more towards our future. I received a little brown envelope every Friday with the cash inside.

Mick had earned quite good money in the merchant navy, but he said he was tired of going away to sea, so he went for an interview to be a post office engineer, and got the job. Nowadays they are known as British Telecom. He started as a junior and gradually worked his way up. We were saving money to put a deposit on a house. We reckoned we would have enough in another year, so it seemed a good idea to get married; I would be nineteen, and Mick would be twenty-one.

But when we told our parents it didn't go down well. Now that I am older and wiser, I realise that Dad, having only just emerged

31

from bankruptcy, was strapped for cash, but I never gave it a thought. I was floating along in a magical dream, and couldn't wait to get married. Mick's parents also felt we should wait for three years until I was twenty-one. Mum was the only one who seemed to understand. My dad thought I was far too young, and the more he and Mick's parents opposed it, the more we both wanted to get married. Dad became even more difficult as my nineteenth birthday approached. Because I was under twenty-one, I had to have the signature of one parent and Dad flatly refused to sign, and for the first time ever, my mum opposed him and signed. I expected my dad to be very upset about that, but my mum had spoken to him, and whatever she said must have changed his mind because all the arrangements went ahead, and he said he was looking forward to giving me away. He hugged me as he said it, so I don't think he meant it in any way other than love.

So the wedding was booked for September 21st 1963. It was being held at St John's Church, the banns were read, and Mum and I went shopping to buy my wedding dress. We found a beautiful one, simply cut with a high neck. It was a perfect fit, and nobody knew we had bought it at a half price sale. I would imagine that nowadays brides with a budget get their wedding dresses online. I was very happy with it, and the headdress and veil that came with it.

Mick had asked his brother Roger to be best man, and Roger's girlfriend Yvonne already had peach bridesmaid's dresses from another wedding, which she kindly loaned to us for the day, so she was one bridesmaid and Sylvia was the other, and we bought them both some new fancy shoes to match the outfit.

We wanted to make Ron feel included, so he was the usher, showing people to their seats in the church. We used our own cars, adorned with white ribbons, and the reception for the thirty guests invited was being held at our house. Mum dismissed any suggestions of hiring caterers, she did the food herself, and did us proud. We bought only the wedding cake.

It had been raining earlier in the morning, but the sun came through in time for us. When dad came in the car with me, he was careful to help me with the long skirt of my wedding dress, as there were still puddles. Everything went off very well, and at home afterwards the informal wedding reception was full of relatives and close friends who all wished us well in our future life together. Howard's mother also came and she gave me a white Bible as a present.

When we had been looking at houses, we realised that living at Shirley, or Purley, which was where Mick came from, was not an option, we needed to find a home in a less expensive area.

We had found a house in Redhill, close to the railway line. It had a controlled tenant living in it; a widower in his seventies. As the house, which was an end of terrace, was very old and needed a lot of work doing to it, it was only £1,500. Mick was very enthusiastic about doing it up and modernising it, but our elderly neighbour wanted everything downstairs left exactly as it was, he loved his outside toilet, scullery and wooden draining board. We offered to put him in a new bathroom, but he said he liked using his tin bath by the fire, and as for central heating, he didn't want any of that modern nonsense!

So we just concentrated on the upstairs. I had a new fitted kitchen and a bathroom, the two bedrooms were decorated, the front one with the big window became our lounge, and the one at the back of the house was our bedroom. We had managed to start our married life with our own home, and at that point in our lives, the upstairs flat was perfectly big enough for us.

Well 1963 was a happy year for us; the start of our married life together, and our future stretched out invitingly.

Chapter Four

For the first year I travelled from Redhill to Croydon with a car share, as one of the men in my office lived in Redhill. We left early every day, getting back at past six o'clock every evening. This meant that although I lived in Redhill, I was only there at weekends, so I decided to get a job in a local shop.

On 10th March 1964, our Queen gave birth to her fourth, and last child. He was named Prince Edward, and is now known as the Duke of Wessex.

I was now twenty years old, and one of my friends was having her twenty-first birthday party. A lot of people were going, and it was going to be held in a local hall. I was excited about it, as I would be meeting up with quite a few of my girl friends that I hadn't seen for a while. Mick's friends would be there too. A small band had been hired for the occasion, and the host was organising party games.

We were put into two groups and given general knowledge questions. The first one with the right answer had to run up to the stage and tell the host, and claim the prize, which was a box of chocolates. I whispered what I thought was the answer to my team, they agreed it was right, and Mick in his excitement gave me a push so I would get to the stage quickly.

I slid along the polished wooden floor and my stiletto heel caught in an uneven piece, and I went crashing headlong against the stage. I didn't remember any more, as I passed out, and when I came round I was propped onto a chair, surrounded by a concerned group of friends. Mick was saying how sorry he was, but I felt like I was floating in a sea of pain. My face felt like it was on fire, and although I was aware of them all around me, panic rose inside me, as I couldn't see anyone. I heard their voices; someone was saying I needed to go to hospital, and I remember thinking that I had come to a party, I wasn't drunk, and yet this horrendous accident had happened. I wondered why I couldn't see. I was so scared.

At the hospital they did their best to patch me up, and I was given painkillers. The doctor warned me that my face was badly bruised, my left eye was swollen and going black, which was why I couldn't see, and my right eye had also gone black and closed up in sympathy with it. I was taken home, and the party came to a premature end, which was a shame. By the next day the shock had come out, and I was shaking and sweating, and had to stay in bed for several days. I don't think my poor husband could bear to look at me; he felt so bad, but it had been a genuine accident, and mirrors were kept away from me for a few days.

To our horror, the doctor had said it might take several months for my face to heal up, and I might even have to go to a hospital at East Grinstead which specialised in plastic surgery. I couldn't believe what I was hearing, nor could Mick. I knew I would have to leave my job at the shop, so he went and explained why to them. They did say I was welcome to return when I felt better, even if it did take a little while, which was so kind of them, but by then I found myself in a deep depression that I couldn't seem to fight.

Mick had to go off to work each day, and I was at home on my own. I didn't want to go out and face people. My face looked like I had been in a fight, and it took a month before my sight came back. When it did come back, the first thing I did was look in a mirror. That was a big mistake, my eyes had purple bruises underneath them, and there was a livid raised purple bruise on my cheek. For a while I shut myself away from a world I felt was full of curious faces and rude stares. I wouldn't even go shopping. Mick felt desperate, he said I had lost my spark, and I had; I was only twenty years old, and my face was scarred. Then he had a good idea; he brought home a puppy.

Tina was a sweet little collie puppy, and she really did help me to pick up my life. I went outside again to walk her, she was my constant companion all day long. I stopped thinking about myself, and concentrated on her. But by the time she was six months old, she had started to have fits. Mick had bought her from a pet shop, which is what people did in the 1960s, but no one would do that now. Our vet told us she was frail and a fit might take her off, but if she reached a year old, then she might have a future.

I felt heartbroken about that. I was beginning to accept that my face would always be marked, but at least I was still alive. After six months, I had to go to East Grinstead hospital for a follow-up appointment, to see if they could do anything more to help me. After a lot of debate, the surgeon explained that I had chipped a bone in my cheek, but he felt as it was such a sensitive spot, any sort of plastic surgery would leave a scar which would be worse than the bruise I still had.

I had by now got used to what I referred to as 'the dent in my cheek.' By the time I celebrated my twenty-first birthday the next year, the bruise had finally healed and I was left with a slight line, which I didn't worry about, it looked a bit like a dimple. The most important thing which I was truly grateful for, was that my eyes healed up, and my sight came back.

On 24th January 1965, Sir Winston Churchill, probably the greatest orator we have ever had, passed away. His body lay in state, and it seemed right to go and pay our respects to him, so Mick and I, together with Tony and his wife Janet, made the journey to London to file past his coffin together with so many others. The crowds were huge, and the respect for this man was very apparent.

In April my mum and dad threw a twenty-first birthday party for me at home with all my friends and family around me, and it was lovely. I had conquered my depression and really felt I had got my life back on track again. Tina reached a year old, and her fits stopped, so that was also very heartening.

In September of that same year, I started to feel very sick and went to the doctor, who said I was most likely pregnant. In those days there were no scans or pregnancy tests, and it was finally confirmed when I was three months. My two friends, Jean and Jenny from Grants, had both married now, and had young children. I was excited to know that Jean was moving to Redhill, so we could spend time together, and our children would grow up knowing each other.

I had severe sickness during my pregnancy; not just for three months, but all the way through. I felt quite wretched most of the time, and went to bed about nine o'clock every night; but my doctor assured me it was only strong hormones and I was carrying a healthy baby. I had been planning to return to work, but as I was now pregnant, it would be hard to get a job just for a few months, so we had to manage on just Mick's wages.

Mick was thrilled about the pregnancy, and he hoped for a boy, and I also thought it would be nice to have a boy. Nowadays couples can be told the sex of their baby when they have a scan, but we didn't know until the birth, and that made it even more exciting. Because I was not able to keep much food down, I didn't put on a great deal of weight. I was existing mainly on Lucozade and tonic water; couldn't drink tea or coffee at that time. Nevertheless, the doctor said my baby was growing and it was taking its nourishment from me.

In April 1966 my first born came into the world. When I was told he was a boy I was thrilled, and couldn't wait for Mick to come in and see his new son. In 1966 fathers were not allowed to be present at the birth. My son had beautiful blue eyes and a slight wisp of fair hair, and I marvelled at this 6lbs 7oz baby I had produced. The miracle of birth remains to me the most amazing thing that can happen to a woman; the creation of a new life lovingly carried inside us for nine months, and then the journey from babyhood, then childhood, and finally they become an adult.

We named him James, middle name Ronald after my brother, who is his godfather, but as soon as he was able to say his name it became Jimmy, and we now all call him Jim. I used to religiously take him to the clinic every week to get him weighed, to make sure he was doing OK; I was so anxious to be a good mother and get everything as right as I could.

Jean's son had been born a couple of years before, and she now had a daughter as well, so she was able to give me some helpful tips. I loved being a mum, and my parents, and Mick's, were very proud grandparents. Because I had been so thin, my pregnancy hadn't been very noticeable, and after Jim was born I was breastfeeding him, so the bit of extra weight I had carried came off very quickly. When I returned to the doctor for my postnatal examination my weight was seven and a half stone, and he complained that I was too thin, and must try and put some weight on, especially as I was breastfeeding. It was a relief not to feel sick any more, and I was enjoying my food once again, but I still couldn't seem to put any weight on. I am smiling as I write this, because I resigned myself to being skinny all my life, not realising how hard it would be to keep weight off when I got older.

When Jim was three months old, two events occurred which stand out in my mind. I had the TV on whilst I was feeding him, and although not a huge football fan, Great Britain had reached the semi-finals of the World Cup, so I watched the match; and was so thrilled to see us win!

We had realised that now we had a baby, our flat would soon become too small, and although the estate agent warned us it might be hard to sell with a controlled tenant in, we put it up for sale. Another young couple, starting off in the same way as we had, wanted it, and we did actually make a profit, which enabled us to buy a semi-detached house in a very pretty tree-lined side road opposite a primary school. The house was situated on a bend, so we had a nice front garden, and a small back garden which was not overlooked. Round the corner was a recreation ground, which we could see from a bedroom window. It had three bedrooms, the kitchen was a fair size, and Mick used his handyman skills to make the two downstairs rooms into a big through room with foldaway doors to separate them when needed, and we also had a serving hatch from the kitchen.

After we had been there about a week, Mick went back to work. I had just got myself ready to go and see Jean, who only lived a couple of roads away, and fed Jim, who was now in his pram, and there was a knock at the door. When I opened it, I was amazed to see Howard. He had disappeared when I became engaged, some four years earlier, even his mother wasn't sure where he was, and now he had suddenly turned up out of the blue.

I welcomed him in and made him a cup of coffee, and he was a perfect gentleman. He admired Jim and our new home, asked after Mick, and told me I looked positively blooming, and how much motherhood suited me. He was even more handsome in his early twenties, but no longer did my heart flip when I saw him; my teenage crush had run its course. When he said goodbye to me he hugged me and told me he was starting a new life in America. I am not sure where he had got my new address from, but as it was him who had found me again, I suggested that we keep in touch with Christmas cards, and asked him to send me his new address when he settled.

Whether he did go to America I am not sure, because I never heard from him again. I truly hope he managed to find the happiness he deserved to have. I will always remember him as my first true love, and then as a dear friend. Over the years I also lost touch with his mother, but will always remember her with fondness; she was a kind lady. Memories become very precious as life goes on, and I was only just beginning to make mine.

Chapter Five

There is something really special about your first child. The feeling of being a new mother, learning how to cope with this helpless little being, and the feeling of pride that you and your partner created him. I used to touch his tiny fingers and toes when he was sleeping, marvelling that he was perfect.

When Jim was a year old, I became pregnant again. This pregnancy was also a sick one, and again the months seemed interminable to me. The baby was due in January, and just after Christmas I had 'flu. As it was my second baby, the doctor had said I could have it at home, but the weather worsened and the snow arrived. It was decided I should go to hospital as, if there were any complications, it might be difficult for the ambulance to get through.

This was a long and complicated labour; it lasted for three days. They were getting concerned that my baby's heartbeat was getting weaker, which sounded very scary, but as soon as my daughter was born, she proved to be strong and healthy, with a weight of 6lbs 15ozs. She looked similar to her brother with wispy blonde hair and blue eyes. We had already chosen her names; Anita Jane. Life felt so good to me, a boy and a girl, and it felt like our family was complete.

Jimmy and Anita were always very close; there was twenty months between them, but they almost seemed like twins. They did most things together, and I had a double buggy to take them out in. Jim had always been a fairly quiet child, but Anita was the complete opposite. She started to pronounce her words at the age of a year, and was using sentences very shortly afterwards. She was never still, and into everything, more than Jim had ever been. She questioned everything, but of course that is how a young child learns. She had a lot more to say for herself than Jim, and often spoke for him, telling us what he wanted.

One particular evening in 1969 sticks in my mind. It was a Wednesday; for Mick it was darts night, he belonged to a club, and they met up once a week. Once I had got my little ones off to bed, I sat watching TV whilst doing my knitting. I enjoyed knitting all their little cardigans and jumpers. On a Wednesday evening there was a programme called 'Gangsters', which I really liked watching, and usually Tina lay by my feet. This was her time with me when the children were in bed. I was so busy with them during the day she had to take a back seat, but she didn't seem to mind, unlike when I had first had her before the children were born.

But earlier in the day she had been sick. I bought some chicken for her, as I thought if I cooked it with some rice, it might be more digestible for her. I had made up my mind that if she was still being sick the next day, I would take her to the vet and get some medication for her. She lay at the other end of the room, flopped out, and I thought maybe she was hot and had moved back to cool off. I spoke to her, telling her she was my lovely girl, and although she remained flopped, her tail thumped against the floor.

I hoped that meant she was feeling better, and turned my attention to the TV. But within a couple of minutes, she made a deep rasping sound as she breathed; I looked over and saw her body jerk, and her eyes became staring and lifeless. A sixth sense told me my dear dog had just died. I wished Mick was there because I didn't know what to do.

So I was now feeling very panicky, I didn't want to believe I had lost my little girl dog; she was only five years old, and I didn't realise that being sick would cause her to die. I ran to the house of my neighbour opposite; a kindly middle-aged lady with two teenage sons.

She could see I was in deep distress, so she came over with me and took charge of the situation by making me a cup of tea after carefully covering Tina's body with a coat. I said I didn't know what time Mick would be back, but she didn't mind, she stayed with me until he came in.

When our vet came the next day to take our little Tina for cremation, I burst into tears and told him that it was all my fault because I hadn't brought her to the surgery after she was sick. He was so kind, insisting I was not to blame; even if I had taken her, she was not a strong dog, and unable to fight against gastroenteritis.

Three months after Anita was born, I took the children out on a bus, and when it stopped I struggled so much with the push chair and holding my little ones, it made up my mind. I would learn to drive.

I passed my test at the second attempt; unlike my friend Jean, who had taken five attempts. She joked about it, and when she finally passed she wore a very colourful trouser suit, which the examiner commented on. She laughed and said he was so busy admiring that, he hadn't watched her driving, and so she had passed. She was in fact a completely safe driver, and I think her failures were down to nerves on the day.

We only had one car between us, but if I needed it that day, I would drop Mick off at the depot, and then pick him up in the evening. Now that I was driving, it gave me much more freedom to go out visiting with the children.

When Anita was just a few months old, Mick and I were sad to hear that a married couple who were friends of ours had parted. We were godparents to their daughter, who was by then five years old. They asked us if we could foster her for a while, as they were both living somewhere that was not suitable for children.

I was happy to do that because I was very fond of her, and thought how devastating it must be for her to be away from both her parents. She stayed with us for about six months, and being older, she used to help me when we went out in the car, by sitting in the back and keeping Jim happy. Anita was in a carry cot, which of course in those days was just on the back seat, and she slept a lot. Later on my god-daughter went to live with her grandmother, who brought her up.

In 1970, when Jim was four and Anita was two, I became pregnant again. It wasn't a planned pregnancy. I found looking after my two little ones exhausting, and to make matters worse, Mick had signed himself up for call-out, which meant he could be called to work to do a breakdown at any time of the day or night. Many family visits had been ruined, and the odd evening out that we had, cancelled at the last minute. I was left to explain to parents who thought they were coming over to babysit, that we were not going out. I know he did it with the best of intentions, the extra money would help towards things we needed, but at that time I didn't see it that way. I needed some support with the children, and he wasn't there to help me. He must have known it would upset me, as he had accepted the call-out job without even telling me about it.

Luckily for me, this pregnancy was not a sick one. I felt very well this time, and as time went on, I was looking forward to welcoming our new addition; and Jimmy and Anita were very excited about having a baby brother or sister.

In February 1971 Britain embraced decimalisation. We now had to forget about the pounds, shillings and pence we had learned at school; and food prices were raised without us even realising, whilst we got used to the new money.

Jim was five by now and due to start school; luckily it was just across the road. I took him over there, and was surprised to see him come back on his own at lunchtime. I took him back, and it turned out that the teacher had told the class to go out, at playtime, and Jim had taken it literally. He settled in OK at school, although he did miss Anita. They used to fight over toys, but she didn't want to play with them without him. After he had been at school for a week the teacher asked us to go and see her. When we got there, she mentioned that they were concerned about Jim's lack of speech. I said he had a very chatty sister, but his teacher suggested Jim had speech therapy.

So he had speech therapy and it really helped him. He was by nature quiet, with never a lot to say. He had previously been at playschool a couple of mornings a week, and the teachers there had always been very complimentary about him, saying how interested in cars he was, and how well he played if left to his own devices.

Mick did more and more call-outs to help pay for the new arrival, and I coped as best I could. The call-outs were at the weekend, and on one particular Saturday my friend had taken Jimmy and Anita to Brighton for the day, and I was going to go food shopping and then have a rest in the afternoon. I was two weeks away from my due date, and Mick had gone off to work early that morning.

I went and got my shopping; then cooked myself some sausages for lunch, as I fancied a sausage sandwich. I was glad to sit down, and I must have dozed off after that, because I woke up with a start when I felt a pain shoot through my stomach. It wasn't a huge pain; it felt like indigestion, and I berated myself for having the sausages. After managing to contact my doctor, he told me that he was on duty at the local hospital, and if I came up there he would give me something safe to ease my indigestion.

I drove myself up there after leaving Mick a note in case he came home and wondered where I was. But when I arrived my waters broke; my baby was on its way, and I was totally unprepared for it. I don't remember the birth being that painful; it all happened so quickly, Philip was born only an hour after my waters had broken. But when I held my baby boy in my arms nothing else seemed to matter. I had hoped for another boy; he weighed 6lbs 14ozs, and he resembled Jim and Anita with his very blue eyes and white blond hair.

Jimmy and Anita were so thrilled to have a baby brother, and they liked to help me by fetching nappies or rocking the pram, which touched my heart. I was able to breastfeed again, and we soon settled back into a routine.

But less than six weeks after Phil was born, I woke up one night with excruciating stomach pains. I sat up in bed; Mick was sleeping, and I could feel sweat pouring off me, and this pain rolling round my stomach was absolute agony. Mick woke up to hear me screaming. I was crouched on the floor with my knees drawn up to my stomach, desperately trying to find some relief.

But nothing could help me, so he telephoned for the doctor. Appendicitis was diagnosed, and I was taken to hospital by ambulance. When the ambulance came, my doctor had said that Mick must take over with Phil and put him on formula milk, but I was having none of that, my baby was not going to be parted from me at such a young age, so he came with me in the ambulance.

I was operated on early the next morning, and when I woke up later, my throat felt very dry, my stomach was aching, and I felt very weak. I was advised to not feed Phil until the next day, and they gave him formula, which he promptly vomited back. So I did what I thought any mother in that situation would do, I breastfed him. My milk was temporarily a bit sparse, but he did settle afterwards. After that nobody told me what to do; I think they decided I wouldn't listen anyway, but my baby was my priority. Gradually my milk came back, and I became stronger over the next few days; maybe a bit slower than I would have done if I wasn't breastfeeding, but such was my determination that my baby wouldn't suffer. Doctors explained that I had been a very interesting case. My womb had not gone back to its normal size after the pregnancy because it was too early, and for my appendix to rupture at such a time was something they had never encountered before. It was believed that my appendix must have been grumbling for months, but I had not been aware of it.

I was in hospital for ten days, and I missed Jimmy and Anita very much. It had been playing on my mind that when I had been taken from the house on a stretcher, writhing in agony, and quite vocal about it, they had been woken up by the noise and had seen me, which must have been very distressing for them. But I needn't have worried, Mick brought them to see me, and they were as lively as ever, especially when I told them that Phil and I would be home with them very shortly.

When I got home, my doctor had arranged for Anita to go to a council run playschool for a couple of weeks. Jim was at school luckily, to give me a chance to get back on my feet. I was very grateful for that help, so I could concentrate on just myself and Phil.

Within a few weeks I noticed that Phil was different from my other two children; he was content with his own company. I used to put him out in the garden to get fresh air, as all mothers did in those days, and when he woke up after a sleep he would kick his legs and watch the branches moving, making gurgling noises. He would have done that all day if I let him, but when I went out to pick him up out of the pram he became angry and roared at me, and because I was feeling quite sensitive at this time, I felt as though my baby didn't love me. I told Mick how I felt, and he must have assumed I was just suffering from the baby blues, which hadn't been helped by the fact that I had just had an operation. A feeling of something not being right was growing inside me.

Phil was always a good feeder, that was never a problem, so he continued to put on weight. I noticed one day that he had a tiny red spot under his eye, so I took him to the doctor. I was then referred to the hospital, who confirmed it was a birthmark, or naevus, and it would continue to grow with his face until he was about a year old, and after that would become less significant. I was to take him to the hospital once a month so they could check that it didn't grow up and block his sight.

In the autumn of 1971, my parents realised a dream by selling their house and moving to a bungalow in Herne Bay. Dad had about four years left before he retired, but he was happy to get the train up to County Hall every day, and back again to Herne Bay in the evening. During the October half term I came to stay with them for a week. I was pleased and excited for them, and I knew the children would love going to visit them in their new home. Mick couldn't get time off work, but the children had a good time; we went for walks along the promenade every day.

The next year was a very difficult one. Firstly Phil developed eczema; it was really bad, dry patches of skin everywhere, and they wept when he scratched them. I had to bind his hands in mittens to stop him from making himself bleed. By the time he reached a year old, he was still lying on his back with no great interest in the world around him. The hospital were of the opinion that this was because he didn't feel very well, so he wasn't progressing, but instinctively I knew that something was wrong and I said so, but nobody, including Mick, took any notice of me.

Anita was now three years old and she went to playschool three mornings a week, so I just had Phil at home with me. I tried to hide my depression; I was so worried about Phil, and it probably didn't help my marriage as I was so wrapped up in my children.

The doctors had been right about Phil's birthmark; it reached its maximum size when he was a year old, it glared vividly across his cheek, and I became fed up with people in the street commenting about it whenever I went out in public with him. My friends, who already knew him, were polite, but strangers just didn't care, or maybe didn't think how their comments might hurt.

In 1973 Phil had his first asthma attack. It was so frightening seeing him struggling for breath, his lips were blue, and his face grey. We were visiting my parents at the time, and he was rushed to Canterbury Hospital. Nebulisers had not been invented then, and he was put in an oxygen tent. They looked after him very well, and after a few days, we were able to take him home. I couldn't help remembering my sister who died, and it was scary.

I received a letter inviting me to take Phil to Great Ormond Street Hospital for various tests. He was now two years old, with very delayed development; just starting to sit up, but his back seemed to be very stiff. It was whilst he was in there that I learned to count my blessings, because no matter how hard life seems to be at times, if you look around yourself, you can always find someone who is worse off.

The first example of this was when I heard a baby gurgling and looked into the cot; this poor little mite gave me the most dazzling of smiles, but his poor little arms and legs were all bent up and twisted. He didn't seem to be in pain, but clearly would never be able to use his limbs.

"That poor baby, it's so sad." I said to the nurse, and she agreed, saying he didn't have much to smile about, but was still a happy baby.

"His parents live in Wales, so they can't visit that often," she added, and I felt like I should wrap him in a blanket and take him home with me; if ever a baby needed love he did.

Phil had all sorts of tests; blood tests, urine tests, then an ECG, everything was carefully analysed, and then after about two weeks we were called into the consultant's office for the results.

"Your little Philip has severe learning difficulties and autism," he said gently.

I had already known about the learning difficulties, and nobody had listened to me. At last, at the age of two years, it had been officially confirmed. But autism, I had no knowledge about that, or what the word even meant.

"What is autism?" I asked.

"It's a physiological condition that some babies are born with; they have difficulty interacting with other children and even with their family, and having learning difficulties makes it even harder for Phil. I am sorry."

I glanced towards Mick, who looked positively wretched, he had always pushed the idea of Phil having learning difficulties out of his mind. I felt a huge wave of guilt; I had carried and given birth to him, it was my fault.

"What can we expect? Will he walk and talk?" he asked desperately.

47

The consultant dodged the question and continued:

"We have done lots of tests to ascertain why Philip has learning difficulties, and we have no definite answers, but after re-examining blood tests that you had during the pregnancy, we have noted that the one you had at eight months contained certain antibodies that were not present at your three months blood test. It is possible in the early stages of pregnancy you may have had German Measles, which then affected your unborn foetus."

I stared at him, amazed, trying to remember back; but I had felt so well this time. I felt at that moment that life was so cruel. Why my son, why anyone's?

He then went on to explain that Phil's limbs were undeveloped because he hadn't used them, and he was going to write to our doctor to suggest that Phil had physiotherapy at the local hospital to strengthen and encourage them. We thanked him and left the room; it all felt so hopeless, and I went back to collect Phil from the ward whilst Mick went to get himself a coffee.

On my way along the corridor, I spotted a lady coming out of a ward with a boy in a wheelchair. He clearly couldn't speak, but was making gesticulations with his arms at her. He looked about ten, but he had lost so much weight that his poor wasted limbs were like matchsticks. She smiled at me, introducing her son who was trying to smile, but movements of any sort were so hard for him, and my heart went out to them both. We fell into step, and she asked me if I had a child in the hospital.

"Yes, I have just been told that Phil has severe learning difficulties and autism." I said, trying not to sound sorry for myself, as she clearly had a very sick son.

"Don't give up on him; while there is life there is always hope!" she said passionately, and I saw the tears in her eyes as she spoke about her son.

"Six months ago he was leading a normal life and playing football, but every day now he gets weaker; his brain cells are dying, but I still have him and I am making the most of every moment!"

I was so moved by her courage in the face of such heartbreak; it made our troubles seem so much less, at least Phil didn't have a sentence of death hanging over him.

"We won't give up; he is having physio to help him walk."

"Good, and now you are going for a walk young man," she

said firmly to her son, and briskly wheeled him away, but with tears in her eyes.

I wondered how she was coping, watching her beloved son declining every day. It certainly gave me a kick up the pants to stop feeling so sorry for myself. Yes there was going to be a difficult path ahead with Phil, but it was up to me, his mother, to weather it. My son was surrounded by love, and I truly believed that love can conquer everything, so I returned to his ward with a new determination inside me. I just wanted to take him home and be with the family.

Great Ormond Street Children's hospital is renowned for the care it gives to sick children, and for every heartbreaking story, there is an uplifting one. When I reached the ward where Phil was in his cot, the curtains were drawn in the bay next to him, but not tightly. I heard a consultant say to a mother, "Let's see what little Ben can do now." A little boy of about three took a few steps and toppled into his arms. I will never forget the look of pride that passed between the mother and the doctor, who had obviously helped this child to walk. If they can do it, we can too, I decided.

c

Chapter Six

So I took Phil to the local hospital every afternoon for physiotherapy. But it didn't go well. He didn't like being touched, so he roared with anger all through the sessions. I found out later that recoiling from touch is quite common for anyone with autism. The nurses were so patient with him, and all I could do was to look on in anguish. After a week or so they explained that they felt it was doing more harm than good, as Phil just tensed his body and refused to co-operate.

I was not in the mood to be defeated, so after I took him home I thought about it. There was one person who had always touched Phil, and that was me. Ever since he had been born he had been handled by me; feeding, dressing and bathing him, and he didn't object. Mick also handled him a little; because he couldn't walk, he used to carry him up on his shoulders if he wasn't in his pushchair.

So I started to work on him. I sat him on my lap and rubbed his limbs as they had done, and in the beginning he grumbled a little, but not as loudly as he had at the hospital. Whenever I had a few spare minutes during the day I sat down with him; and it became a normal routine, and he stopped flexing his body against me and started to relax. He was sitting much better now, his back was stronger, and one day he found he could get across the floor on his bottom. He never did crawl; this went on for over two years, and he went through the seat of a great many pairs of trousers.

In the meantime, Jim was due to go to middle school, and we were called in to speak to the head. Because he was late speaking,

50

and didn't speak up or question anything in class, it had held him back and he was struggling, but they believed that if he went to a school with smaller classes he would manage very well.

Initially I balked at the idea. I was already ostracised by some mothers at the school because Phil had difficulties; they seemed to think that if their children came to play at our house they might catch something. This may sound unbelievable, but back in 1973 not enough was known about children with difficulties; they got stared at in the street, and comments were made, and some families never took them out, they were hidden away because Mum was made to feel ashamed. Just because Jim had started off with speech problems, I didn't want people to assume he had the difficulties that Phil had because that just wasn't true. He was healthy and his IQ test had shown he had normal intelligence.

I think attitudes have changed because of programmes such as 'Children in Need', and 'Comic Relief', where the plight of many families in need is seen on our television screens, and the great British public are encouraged to donate to help them. We embrace any sort of disability now, as is only right, and society has deemed we are all equal, and nobody is more glad than I am that this is the case now; but it wasn't the case then.

So in the end I did agree. I decided that if a school with smaller classes would help Jim, then to hell with anyone who looked down on us, they were simply not worth worrying about. Due to our unusual family situation we are very closely knit and loyal to each other, because there were many times when it felt like it was us against the world.

The situation made me realise exactly who my friends were, and I had a few really loyal ones. I was sad that Jean and Alan had now emigrated to Australia on the ten pound scheme. Alan was a carpenter, and felt he could do really well there. Jean had been great fun to be with, and we had known each other since I was sixteen, so I did miss her.

I met a girl called Gill in the local park. She had two boys who were similar in age to Jim and Anita. They were very lively, and I have a smile on my face as I remember her running to catch one of them when he ran away from her, and when she returned she said:

"Oh well, it certainly helps to keep me fit."

Gill and her husband Alan were Welsh, and sometimes when

they were speaking in full flow, I didn't understand everything that they said. Gill used to look after Anita for me when I had to take Phil for hospital appointments. She was a very loyal friend, and when they were five, the children all started school together. When I told her Jim was going to a different school she didn't turn a hair, she just said that as he had been late talking, if it was going to benefit him, then it was a really great idea. I just wished more people could be like her.

Mick and I had grown apart. I couldn't talk to him about my worries regarding Phil; I had too much guilt. I felt I had let him down; to me it seemed all other women managed to give birth to children without autism or special needs, but I had failed. He did lots of overtime; obviously the money was handy, when you have a young family, but maybe he needed to escape from all the trauma and worry at times.

I totally blamed myself for the break-up. I know he would have never left me; he believed that marriage was for a lifetime, and so had I at the time, but the words of my father came back to haunt me questioning if I was too young to know my own mind. I finally admitted to myself that, although I loved him as the father of my children, I was no longer in love with him.

I made plans to leave him, but it seemed impossible. I hadn't worked for several years due to having babies, all the money I had was in our joint account, and it wasn't possible for me to work, even with Jimmy and Anita at school, because I had to take care of Phil. I was full of guilt about taking his children away from him, and very aware how upset Jimmy and Anita would be, especially Anita, who was his princess. However would I cope?

But I had this driving force inside me to change my life, to do my best for my children; they were my whole life, and I knew I had to face up to my responsibilities, and do it properly. So I told Mick of my plans, saying how sorry I was. He questioned how I would cope, and he had a right to, he didn't want the children to suffer. But the more he opposed the idea, the more I was determined to find a way.

I scanned all the papers; I had an idea in my head that if I could find a shop with living accommodation, maybe I could keep Phil with me and work on the premises. I found a wool and haberdashery shop with rented accommodation, and to my delight it was very close to Coney Hall, where I had been so happy as a child.

I went over to visit it. It was in a secondary parade with half a dozen other shops, with the bus stop right outside it. The shop itself was big, and so was the maisonette above it. It had a good sized kitchen, a lounge and dining room, and then up another flight of stairs was the bathroom and three bedrooms. There was a small garden out the back, and parking space.

It all needed updating; the shop and maisonette was in a terrace and probably dated back to the 1930s. I wondered how my children would feel leaving their nice comfortable home with a big garden and a swing to live in a maisonette above a shop.

Mick was surprised when I told him. I think he thought I had gone off the idea because it was so difficult. I had to pay three months rent in advance plus key money, and then the owner wanted £3,000 for the goodwill and fixtures and fittings of the shop.

Nothing had been mentioned about a divorce as yet; I wanted to get Mick used to the idea of separation first. This meant selling our house was not an option. I think he wanted to keep the house anyway, in case I changed my mind and came back, and he didn't want to move into a flat, so he took out a second mortgage, and gave me £5,000.

The day I left I was an emotional mess; guilt, fear of the future, and many emotions raged around my insides. Mick went off to work as usual, but he knew I would not be there when he got home. I had arranged for Jimmy and Anita to change to local schools. The new school for Jim was walking distance from the shop, and I had met the staff and felt comfortable in the knowledge that he would be happy there.

I had hired a van driver for the beds and children's things I was taking, and they had charged me £25, but when they unloaded he was grizzly saying he hadn't known that there were two flights of stairs, so he wanted another £5. I gave it to him, and then looked around me. It had been a very long day, and I now had beds to make up. The children were excitedly running about, seemingly unaware of the shabby outdated decor. I had arranged for them to go back and stay with Mick the following weekend, hoping that would soften the parting from their dad.

When my parents and Ron heard what I had done they were devastated. My mum and dad believed you married for life, and faced all that life throws at you together, just as they had, and that made me feel even more guilty. They were both very fond of Mick, and they couldn't see how I would manage as a single mother with the added difficulty of Phil having special needs. On more than one occasion they urged me to return to him, and stop 'being silly.'

But their negativity only made me want to prove I could cope. I opened the shop two days after we had moved in, after getting the children settled into their new schools. Anita had already made friends with a girl called Linda in her class, and they remained friends even after they left school. Her mother Audrey became my close friend. Audrey had an amazing sense of humour, and we had many laughs together over the years.

On the first evening, after all the children were in bed, I went downstairs to the shop to survey the scene. I had bought the stock together with the goodwill, there was knitting wool, patterns, all types of haberdashery, including a big old chest with many drawers containing buttons of every shape and colour. They could be bought singly, and over the years, many people came in to search through those drawers for the right size and colour.

There were also a few items of nightwear and underwear by brand names, suitable for the older lady; apparently there were some regulars in the area who preferred to buy locally. But I didn't want to just appeal to one age group, I wanted people of all ages to come into my shop, so I planned to include children's clothes at a later date. In the meantime I found a couple of ladies dresses, a little bit dated, but I put them on the models, then added a basket of balls of wool in all colours. I temporarily put my old sewing machine in the window, and ranged useful items of haberdashery around it, with another basket on the table with items such as hand cream, soap, tissues, and all the things we tend to run out of during the week, nestling inside. It might not sound very exciting, but it started me off very well. The lady who had owned the shop before had reached retiring age and lost interest, and the window had not been changed for months.

Local people popped in and introduced themselves, and I began to feel like part of a community, and I liked that, and I kept a suggestions book, and when customers asked for certain items, I did my best to stock them.

As far as Phil was concerned, my idea worked. Behind the counter was a door which led to an area at the back, and there was also a cloakroom with a toilet. I made that area completely childproof, it was like a big playpen, and I had a gate so that he couldn't get onto the shop floor. Phil was mad about Matchbox cars. Jim had passed quite a few over to him that he had played with himself, and Phil would spend ages meticulously lining them up; sometimes a whole day. So I was able to keep him safe, and work in the shop all day. Sometimes I tucked him up for a nap on the sofa after lunch. I also had a portable TV in there and a record player, as Phil has always loved music.

It took about three months before my takings were enough to feed us and pay the rent, I brought in children's knitwear, and then dresses. Often parents will spend on their children rather than themselves. What was popular with little girls at that time were skirts with elasticated waists and a frill at the bottom. So in the evening, when I had a bit of spare time, I got out my sewing machine, and used some of the floral material from some ladies dresses that hadn't sold because they were out of date. With a bit of broderie anglaise around the frill, they were transformed, and it cost me almost nothing. I used to put a hanging rail out with them on to tempt passers by and anyone standing at the bus stop.

I also found a local lady who did knitting and crochet, and she made some beautiful baby jackets and cardigans, and they also went well. I had to work every moment of every day, except Sunday, which gave me some time to spend with the children. But this one day off wasn't enough, so I put a notice on the door and closed on Mondays as well. Some other shops in the parade also did this, so it made sense to me to get in line with them, rather than have a half day on a Wednesday which a few of the shops did. Half a day off was never enough, and closing on a Monday seemed to work well.

Sometimes on a Monday I would go to the warehouse to pick out stock that I wanted. One of my very necessary purchases had been a car; I couldn't have managed without one, so I had a second hand black Ford which I hoped would keep going long enough until I could afford something better. Phil had a car seat and he enjoyed riding in the car, so I took the fold-up buggy and transferred him into it whilst I walked around deciding what I thought I could sell.

One Monday during the school holidays, I decided I would take the children out shopping to Bromley, and we would also have lunch out as a treat. I was proud of my children; they had been brought up to sit at the table and not get down until they had eaten; even Phil sat nicely waiting for his lunch, so I knew they would behave when we went out, and they certainly deserved some of my time, as recently I had spent so much of it in the shop. Audrey had also been a godsend, she came in after school with Linda. Anita and Linda played upstairs, and she helped me in the shop or made tea if I was busy, and she wouldn't take a penny for doing it.

So life seemed to be getting easier. My family were still not convinced that I was doing the right thing, nor Mick, but I clung on stubbornly to the new life I had created for us. It was Easter holidays, the Monday before Good Friday, and whilst we were in Bromley, I took them into McDonald's, which was fairly new, but catching on rapidly.

It was full of people, and I suggested they sat down at the table and Jim would help me to bring the order back. Anita sat with her arm around Phil. Her protectiveness towards him was touching to see, as she was only five herself. We queued up to get the order, and then took it to the table; then a voice spoke to me.

"Hello Carol, how are you doing?"

There at the next table was John. I already knew him; he worked with Mick, a good looking young man with very nice manners, he was married with two daughters.

"I am fine thanks, and you?"

I wondered if Mick had told him we had broken up. I wasn't sure, and I felt a bit awkward. It was surprising that he was in Bromley, as he lived in Old Coulsdon, and Croydon would have been nearer for him. But his next words explained everything.

"I am living in South Croydon now at my mum's until I find something. My wife and I have split up."

"Oh, I am so sorry. We are living in West Wickham for the same reason."

His eyes showed empathy. He had always struck me as a kind man, and I knew he was a devoted father, so it must have been hard for him to go. I think my revelation was new to him; which didn't surprise me, as I wasn't sure Mick would tell his work mates, because he had been expecting me to come back, as he didn't think I would cope.

I then went on to tell him about the shop, and how it fitted in with my new life. He was very tactful, and didn't ask anything about our break-up. Jim and Anita had by now spotted some friends, and asked if they could go over and say hello to them. So whilst they were gone I found myself telling him about Phil's delayed development, and how I was trying to help him to walk, but so far he hadn't got any further than crawling around on his bottom.

"Never mind, Phil will grow up just like the others," he said brightly, which I found very heartening.

Talking to him had been nice, as it had been mainly me and the children for the last three months. As we departed I gave him my address and said he was welcome to pop in for a cup of tea when he was passing. I had vowed when I left Mick that my children and I were going to manage just fine, and I didn't have room for another man in my life; it was too complicated, I had too much baggage to inflict on someone else. But having a friend was a different story, someone to have a laugh with, or a moan with, apart from Audrey, and someone who felt as bad as I did about having a failed marriage; we were kindred spirits. So John became my best friend.

Chapter Seven

John's visits to the shop became more frequent. I had stored up so much inside me of my fears and worries about Phil for so long, and kept a bright face on for the sake of my children, so it all came tumbling out.

It was too painful to discuss with Mick. I felt so much I had let him down, which I can now see was ridiculous. We are all born as we are, and we all have to make the best of what we have got, and John made me see this. He said it was much easier for him to discuss Phil with me than it would be for Mick, because he wasn't emotionally involved. He also confided in me about why his marriage had gone wrong, and how sad he was about leaving his girls. He was trying to get access so that he could see them regularly.

He played with the children and we took them to swing parks on a Sunday, and they thought he was fun. But when Mick and John's wife found out, neither were impressed. They had both believed we would come back, and so having met up with each other, they both blamed us for the breakdown of our marriages. It was the same with my parents; I had only been separated for three months and now I had another man. I was utterly irresponsible in their eyes, and my protestations that we were only good friends fell on deaf ears. So I actually felt when our relationship changed, all the negativity had pushed us together.

John helped a lot in the shop; he had a flair for window dressing and a great deal of charm with the customers. It was nice for some of the local women of all ages to come in and find a polite respectful young man serving them on a Saturday morning when I had so many other things to do for the children. It wasn't every Saturday because he also spent time with his daughters, but when it happened, I was truly grateful for his help.

I enjoyed having his strength and positivity to push me on, and I was continuing with my physio with Phil,who had now found he could stand up against a sofa and walk along, but nothing and no one could induce him to let go.

Of course, John's visits were upsetting both of our former partners, and in truth I very quickly found myself falling in love with him. We were guilty of all we had been accused of; so I asked him to move in with me, but not before I had sat down with Jimmy and Anita to explain about him.

"Daddy doesn't like him," said Anita, shaking her head sadly.

I felt a huge pang of guilt, what were we putting them through?

"I like him; he takes us swimming," said Jim, stoutly defending him.

"I am sure it will all be fine in the end," I said firmly. It had to be, because I was beginning to realise how much I wanted this man in my life.

So we became a family unit, and initially it was hard; but he wasn't just a boyfriend, he was my soulmate; nobody would ever understand me the way John did. I would never have been with anyone who didn't care about my children, and I didn't believe that anyone would want to take on all the difficulties that came with me, but John never wavered, he said my children were part of me, and he accepted them willingly.

It wasn't long before I became pregnant. This was a huge shock because John had been told by a doctor he was sterile after having mumps some years earlier; indeed the lack of another child had not helped his marriage. I honestly didn't know if I could cope with another baby. I was still having to carry Phil around, and running the shop and coping with the children took all my energy.

But neither could I have an abortion. John was so over the moon about my pregnancy; it was proof he wasn't sterile, and when he told me he was so proud to have me as the mother of his child, I just had to go through with it.

It was now 1974; writing this in 2019 reminds me just how attitudes have changed, but at that time I didn't want anyone to know that we were not married, nor that my child would be illegitimate, so I assumed the surname of Creasey, and left my other one behind.

My doctor referred me to social services when he realised I was pregnant. He said it was time I had some help with Phil, who was now three years old, and he was offered a place at a special school at Beckenham. We went to see them and were impressed by the caring environment. So we agreed to let Phil go. A minibus came to pick him up every morning, and life was a lot easier for me during this pregnancy.

My family had still not come round to our relationship, although they did keep in touch with me. John now made himself busy modernising and repainting and decorating our upstairs accommodation. Knowing what had happened previously with Phil, my doctor wanted to do a needle test to confirm whether my baby would have any problems. In those days they did not have scans, so I would not know the sex of the baby until it was born. He warned me that there was a small risk of a miscarriage, and I wasn't prepared to take that risk, so I didn't have the test. My baby was due in March 1975, but my pains started a month early and I was admitted to Croydon General Hospital.

The first doctor who examined me said it was too early for my baby to be born, it was too small, so they would give me some medication and send me home. The pains persisted, even after the pills, then my waters broke; but just like her sister before her, Andrea Carol took three days to enter this world, and was born in February 1975 weighing 6lbs 5ozs.

John had been with me all the time, as hospitals now allowed partners to be present. I suppose because she was my last child, I can still remember so vividly the pain just before she was born. I had been given medication, but it built up to such a degree, that for one split second I screamed out that I could take no more, and I felt that death would be a welcome relief; it was at that moment her head emerged. It felt like I was at the end of a long tunnel; I could hear voices in the background urging me to push, and then my daughter was born.

I knew instinctively that she was fine; being a month early meant she had a yellow pallor because she was jaundiced, but the doctors assured me this was not a problem and was quite normal for an eight month baby.

John was absolutely thrilled with her, and so were Jim and Anita. Although only seven years old herself, Anita adored her baby sister, and made herself available to help as much as possible.

Jim had always helped a lot with Phil; at nine years old, he changed nappies and fed him. I never asked either of them, but they loved to be involved. Sometimes on a Sunday, they would get up and change their nappies and dress them, just so I could spend a bit longer in bed. They knew it was my day off from the shop, and they were not at school.

Andrea was a very easy baby. I felt she virtually brought herself up; reaching all her milestones. Before she walked she was always on the floor crawling around where Phil was walking along the furniture, and then one day, at the age of a year, she took her first steps. Phil watched her, and not to be outdone, within a couple of days, he also walked. Out of all my children, seeing Phil walk was probably the most happy and emotional moment for me. It meant my son would not have to spend his life in a wheelchair.

My children all had very different characters. Jim was quiet and thoughtful, whereas Anita was a live wire, never still, very affectionate, and she looked just like me as a child. I could see a lot of myself in her nature, but she was always a confident girl, unlike me; she could shine at a party, and she had loads of friends. I have had to work very hard over the years on my confidence.

Andrea was always a very independent girl. She was popular, and she had so much admiration for her elder sister, that as she grew up, she tried to be like her. Like most sisters they argued; Anita was always neat and tidy, and as they shared a bedroom, Andrea's side of it could only be likened to a tip, whilst Anita's side had everything neatly tidied away.

Although my family had not yet accepted John, I couldn't deprive them of their grandchildren, that would have been cruel, so I took the children to visit them at Herne Bay; usually when John was seeing his daughters, and they had been to the shop on one occasion when he was at work.

On 16th August 1977 it was announced on the radio that Elvis, the King of Rock'n'Roll had been found dead in his bathroom with a suspected heart attack. I knew his health had been failing in recent years, and he had put on weight, but he was only forty-two, and I felt very sad. It was the end of an era. It turned out that he had been suffering from the same illness as his mother, and died at the same age. I had followed him as a fan ever since he burst onto the pop scene in 1958, when I was fourteen. Of course, my dad, as well as many other fathers of teenage girls, did not approve of him or his music. Elvis gyrated his hips whilst performing, but as time wore on, he became not only the King of Rock'n'roll, but also an actor, and I saw all his films.

In that same month, my mum rang up and she said my brother Ron would like to bring her up in the car for a visit, and she added: "We would like to meet John, and I thought maybe we could go to the Italian restaurant in your parade for a meal."

Hope flooded through my heart that they were finally going to accept John, but my dad was conspicuous by his absence, so he was obviously not ready to do the same.

"Oh yes, Mum, that would be lovely. The children have Saturday activities, but they will be there in the afternoon. If we go for our meal after I put them to bed, I am sure I can ask Audrey to keep an eye on them."

John was very nervous about meeting them; he had been painted as a marriage wrecker and a villain, and nothing was further from the truth. I told him to just be himself, I was sure my mum would be won over.

I was a bit shocked when I saw my mum. She had always been a tiny slim person, but it was about six weeks since I had last seen her, and she had lost weight and her face and neck looked gaunt. She was also a bit yellow, and said she was going into hospital shortly as she had jaundice and would be having treatment. She said it lightly, but I could not help worrying.

The first thing my mum did after they arrived was to ask Ron to take her to the local shoe shop. Andrea was running around barefoot; at two years old, it was very difficult to get her to keep anything on her feet. She did have slippers, but never wore them. This made no difference to my mum; she insisted in getting her a new pair, and for that day at least she did wear them.

So later that day we went for our meal in the evening, and it seemed to go very well. John was polite and respectful towards my mum. I watched her carefully, and she seemed to enjoy her meal. Mum always was very careful about what she ate; organic things were just coming into the supermarkets, and she never ate anything that had been sprayed, mostly living on salads and vegetables, fish and chicken, with a little bit of meat occasionally.

Mum and Ron went back to Herne Bay, and I felt we might be a step nearer to a reconciliation. Ten days later she went into hospital. My dad rang me and said on no account to worry, as it was nothing serious. It was the first time in my life I could ever remember my mum being truly ill. She had been battling rheumatoid arthritis for the last few years, and she never gave in, such was her spirit, but now she was in hospital for something else.

She had an operation. I didn't actually know what it was for, neither did my dad, he still mentioned jaundice, and it was a few days before we were allowed to visit. Mum had not been out of bed yet, but was finally allowed visitors.

It was the bank holiday weekend and the weather was hot and sunny, so we decided to take the children to the coast for the day, and then go and visit my mum on the way back. John would sit in the car with the children, and if mum was well enough, they could go in and see her too. I still wasn't sure if John should go in, he had only met her once, and I guessed my dad would be visiting as well. We certainly didn't want any conflict at such a traumatic time.

I went in first on my own. I had planned to take Jim in, but he had managed to get his trousers wet on the beach, and was now sitting in the car in just his swimming trunks, so I didn't think I could take him in with me.

When I saw my mother, I was staggered; she looked even thinner, her tiny frame outlined against the blanket, her face lined with pain, and her voice scarcely more than a whisper. She looked very ill to me. The only good thing was the yellow tinge had gone from her face and her cheeks were now pink.

"Oh Mum, you've got your colour back, thank goodness." I said encouragingly, as I sat in the chair next to the bed.

Her speech was a little slurred; they had obviously given her drugs, and her next words truly surprised me.

"I've had cancer, you know. How can that be with the diet I have, I am so careful!"

"Mum, you can't know that, it was jaundice!"

"I heard the doctor say it, cancer he said!"

I sat holding her hand feeling devastated, and wondering if it was true. In 1977 nobody told a patient or their family if they had cancer; unlike nowadays when sometimes we are told too much. I vowed when I went home to find someone who would tell me the truth.

"How are the children; are they with you?"

"Yes, they've been on the beach all day, and they are a bit grubby. Jim even managed to put his trousers in some water, so he only has his bathing trunks to wear home."

"They are going to try and get me up tomorrow."

"That is good news Mum."

My mum lifted up one of her thin little arms, and I saw her wrist was swollen.

"Look, I showed it to the nurses and they don't know why it's so swollen."

"Oh no, does it hurt?"

"Not really dear, but I do feel weary."

"OK Mum, I will let you have a sleep now. I can't come tomorrow, but I will be back to see you soon."

I have wished many times since that night that I had never spoken those words, as I saw her face change; she looked disappointed. We lived sixty miles away, so I knew I couldn't visit her every day, but I so wish I hadn't told her.

I kissed her goodbye, and she sent her love to her little darlings, as she called them.

"Look after them, and remember me to John," were her last words.

I left the ward, and as I passed the office, I saw the ward sister inside. I knocked on the open door, and she smiled back at me. I went in.

"I have just been to see my mother and she has told me she had cancer."

Sister's face registered amazement.

"Really, and why does your mother think that?"

"She says she heard the doctors discussing it."

There was a pregnant pause whilst sister decided what she was going to say to me.

"Well yes, we did an exploratory examination, and your mother had cancer growing over her liver, but we got it all out."

So it was true; I hadn't wanted it to be, not many people survived cancer in the 1970s.

"But will it come back?"

"We can't say. We have cut away the affected part and made repairs, but she will probably have to be on a special diet."

Fear coursed through me; that little figure laying in the bed didn't look much like the strong and determined mother I had known all my life. I spoke with desperation in my voice.

"Please make her well, she is only sixty-seven."

"We will take good care of her," said the sister as I left the room.

I saw my dad and Ron on the way out, and I told them Mum was sleepy. Dad said they were not going to stop for long. I didn't know whether I should tell him what my mum had said, but in the corridor was not a place to discuss such things. So I returned to the car; the children were all getting a bit fidgety, so John drove home, and I then got them all off to bed.

At home I told John of my fears. I spent a troubled night, and the next morning the telephone rang early. When I picked it up, my father's voice was broken with emotion when he said to me:

"I am very sorry Carol, your mother passed away last night. Whatever are we going to do?"

Chapter Eight

My mother's death was a complete shock to all of us. To me she had always been a strong positive person, and in my mind she was invincible. Sixty-seven seemed much too young to lose anyone; I sobbed my heart out when I realised I would never see her again.

The post mortem showed she had died of peritonitis; the swelling of her wrist had been an indication of this. I am sure these days it would have been spotted, and lots of people can survive cancer, but then the prognosis was not good.

My dad was heartbroken, and I was concerned about Ron; he had always been close to mum, but he seemed to be bearing up. By the time the funeral came round, a week or so later, I had managed to get my emotions under control. My aunt and uncle, who lived nearby in Herne, were very upset, my mum was a special lady who always cared more about others than herself. My aunt shed a lot of tears for her sister at the church service, and I sat between Dad and Ron, as close as I could get to them.

Mick had been invited to the funeral, as my mum had been very fond of him; I greeted him awkwardly. John hadn't been invited; he was looking after the children, as we didn't think a funeral was the right place for them at their young ages.

The refreshments were being served at the house, my Aunty Ena was helping, and I stayed behind after to help clear up. I told her how bad I felt that I had upset Mum so much by leaving Mick, and I hoped it hadn't caused her illness. She assured me it wasn't because of me, saying, "Cancer never discriminates, it doesn't care who it touches."

My dad had been so shocked at losing her so suddenly, he said it had given him a different perspective on life. "I want to meet John. If he's your new partner, then I need to meet him."

"He's a good man Dad, you won't be disappointed."

"Time will tell!" my dad said, still unconvinced. But I knew he would soon realise all his preconceived ideas about John were unfounded, and I am so glad that my mum made that visit to us before she died, as she was making her move to reconcile, and had got on well with John that day.

Just after Mum's death, our landlord sent us a letter to say he was selling the block of shops where we were, and if we wanted to buy ours we could have the freehold for ten thousand pounds. All he wanted was five hundred pounds deposit. In her will, my mum had left the bungalow to dad, and she had left her savings of one thousand pounds to be divided between Ron and myself. It seemed like mum had done her bit to help us own our own home, as without that inheritance we could not have proceeded.

I was by now divorced, but John couldn't get his divorce. Regardless of this I trusted him with my life; so married to each other or not, we bought the freehold in our joint names. He paid the mortgage out of his wages, as well as his other mortgage with his wife, and he also paid support for his girls, so it was up to the shop to pay our other bills, and give us enough money to eat. It was very tight, and John took on an extra job in the evenings going out collecting pools rounds.

Jim was by then twelve and Anita ten, so it wasn't long before I also spent an evening helping with these rounds, and they earned their pocket money by helping too. We alternated to make sure there was always someone at home to look after Phil and Andrea.

Jim had joined the Scouts now, and sometimes went away to camp with them. Anita had been a Brownie, but had shown great promise as a swimmer, and was accepted into Beckenham Swimming Club, where she frequently competed in galas. Anita always had an amazing sense of humour, seeing the funny side of anything, and I could relate to this too, so we shared many chuckles together. I remember going to a gala with her when she was swimming in a school relay team; she was doing the breast stroke, and her leg went well and they were winning, but the girl who did the final leg jumped in too deep, and by the time she had surfaced, the other swimmers were halfway down the pool. Instead of being disappointed, my good natured daughter came over to me and laughed, pulling a face and saying, "Oh well, never mind, we blew that one."

Phil was now seven years old, and for the next few years, his health declined rapidly. He was in and out of hospital with frequent asthma attacks, then he had anorexia and this was closely followed by losing all his hair. The doctor said it happened to anxious people sometimes, and it might never come back. But it did; it grew again thick and mid brown in colour, whereas in the beginning he had fine white blond hair. I have since written his biography entitled *My Life is Worth Living!* in which I describe in detail every illness, how we tried to cope, and how we sometimes got it wrong, and the learning curve that we all experienced.

I had found that it was easier when dealing with all that life threw at me, to have a sense of humour, and not to take life too seriously. We couldn't sit down and worry about whether Phil would ever reach adulthood, we had to just take each day as it came, and try and make it as happy as we could for the whole family.

There was one day when Audrey had come round to see me. Everyone was out except Phil; it was lunchtime, and he was sitting in his chair in the kitchen. She was avidly chatting away to me about something, and I was listening to her and trying to sort out Phil at the same time. I decided to heat up some spaghetti hoops, a favourite of his, so I buttered some bread whilst she was chatting, and then turned off the gas and put the spaghetti in a bowl which I put down beside him.

I turned my attention back to her, after setting the bowl and the bread down next to him on the table. Suddenly I heard a bang, and turned to see the spaghetti hoops dripping slowly down our kitchen wall, which had been recently painted. Without even thinking, I said, "Oh, I don't think he wanted that!" and Audrey doubled up with laughter, saying it was the understatement of the year!

Then there was the supermarket surprise; and my, what a surprise that was! I wanted to go to Sainsbury's; usually I left Phil with one of the family, as I could get round so much more quickly on my own, but it was before Sunday opening had happened, and my cupboards were almost bare. It's so easy these days to order online, and then a friendly smiling man brings your shopping to the door, but none of that existed in the 1980s.

I decided it would be fine to take Phil. He was now too big to sit in a trolley, but he would hold onto the side of it; and I wanted to be nice and organised, so I sat down and wrote a list. I got him in the car and then drove to Sainsbury's. As luck would have it, I managed to find a space not far from the door, and I found myself a trolley. Once inside the door, after searching my purse and pockets, I realised I had left the list on the kitchen table. Should I return to get it? And if I did, would I find another space so near, as Phil has never been a fast walker? I decided to stay, thinking that as I had written it all down, and it was fresh in my mind, I would probably remember it anyway.

In those days, supermarkets used to have floor displays of tins, usually built up to a point in the middle, a bit like a pyramid. Health and safety would never allow it these days. As I turned to look at the cereals and try to remember whether it was Cornflakes or Weetabix, or both, that we needed, I heard the loudest crash ever, and turned to see what was happening. Unbeknown to me, at school Phil had been learning to do a twirl, so what better place to practise it than a supermarket. I watched as, in slow motion, every single tin of baked beans crashed to the floor; then, as well as myself, other people were dashing about attempting to pick them up. If there had been a prize for the one who succeeded in getting them all down, Phil would have won it. To make matters worse, watching us all running about gave my son a fit of giggles, which added to my embarrassment.

I didn't find it funny at the time, but when I told John and the children about it later that day, they all thought it was hilarious. I was still careful not to take Phil in there again!

By the time Phil was seven years old, there had been no sign of any speech, but he always made his needs known by pointing, or sometimes taking us by the hand and leading us to what he wanted. He made noises and laughed, indeed he has a hearty laugh, and a great sense of humour. But there were times when he sat on the floor, unable to make us understand his needs, and wept. This absolutely tore at my heartstrings, so when the speech therapist from his school suggested she should come round to our house, and show both Phil and myself Makaton, the sign language for deaf people, it seemed a really good idea.

She duly arrived with all her papers and instructions, and Phil and I sat down with her in our lounge as she felt he would benefit from being in familiar surroundings.

First of all she made Phil lift his head up and look at her properly, which is always a bit difficult. "Right Phil, these are the signs you make to Mum when you want a glass of orange squash," and she followed up her words with several hand gestures.

Phil grinned, rose from his chair, took my hand and led me to the fridge, opened the door and got out the squash, then pointed to the cupboard where the glasses were kept. The poor lady obviously wasn't expecting that, as she conceded defeat and decided perhaps Phil didn't need Makaton after all to make his needs known. Over the years he has developed his own way of communicating, and we have learned to understand what he is asking for. He now makes his own orange drinks, but what we have to beware of is that he would drink it neat if we didn't make sure that he adds the water.

It was often assumed at that time, that people with special needs and learning difficulties had no intelligence, but although it is obviously limited, we have always found that Phil understands all we say to him. We can be sitting there discussing something without bringing him into the conversation, which I was one day, bemoaning that I couldn't find my slippers anywhere, and Phil left the room, only to return triumphantly with the errant slippers.

After my mum died I wished that I lived nearer to my dad and Ron, as my dad was of the old school; he had never changed a nappy in his life, or tried to cook, and probably never used the washing machine. So for a while I used to go down on a Sunday, cook them some dinner and do some washing; but it was exhausting, because I still had my own family to care for and the shop to run.

So my visits became monthly, and I was surprised one day to open a wedding invitation; it said my dad was going to marry Betty Morgan. Surprised puts it mildly; it was the first I knew about him having a girlfriend, and I wondered if it was a joke. I rang him immediately and rather sheepishly he told me that it was true.

If he thought I was going to judge him for marrying just ten months after losing Mum, he was wrong. I knew how much he cared about her, and I also knew he found it hard to cope alone. Then there was Ron; my mum and dad had promised each other, whoever died first, the other one would see that Ron was OK. Indeed I had promised them both that I would always make sure he was OK when they were both no longer around.

When I heard that he had met Betty at the British Legion, on a Saturday evening when they had ballroom dancing, I felt so happy for him. He was a very fit seventy year old, whereas Betty was in her forties. So John and I went to their wedding; Phil came with us, Jim and Anita were at school and Andrea was at nursery, as it was a weekday. We had to keep Phil off, as we wouldn't have been able to get back in time to meet him from the minibus.

My dad was the sort of man who really needed a partner; then he was complete, and I felt sure that Mum was looking down and wishing him well. I have always got on well with Betty, and she was a very good wife to Dad, and stepmum to Ron. She loved cooking, and was always experimenting with new recipes.

We used to take the children down and spend Sunday with them, about every six weeks. I have always loved Herne Bay; it holds happy memories from the 1950s when my dad built the bungalow, and when I visited with the children and John we used to get down on the beach and enjoy a seaside walk whilst we were there.

Now that Dad and Ron were no longer on their own, I felt relieved, like a burden had been removed from my shoulders. Maybe now life was going to get a bit easier.

Chapter Nine

I always start each new year full of hope and expectation, as I have an optimistic nature. It has been put to the test many times, but I have always tried to look on the bright side, rather than be the voice of doom. But my faith was really put to the test in 1979; sales plummeted, and the shop was not making enough money to support us.

John's wages from BT were stretched to the limit, as he paid our mortgage, and the mortgage on his former home, and maintenance for his two daughters. We took on more pools rounds just to feed ourselves and to help towards the household bills, but we were too proud to tell anyone; we were so determined to manage.

Shops were beginning to stock off the peg affordable dresses, so haberdashery sales were low. It was the same with knitted garments; they could be bought for a fraction of the price of hand knitting them, and Great Britain was going into a recession which lasted into the 1980s. Shops selling 'nearly new' were also springing up and doing very well. We had no money to buy new stock, so we had to think of something to stop us going under.

John came up with an idea and immediately put it into action. Our shop was very long, so he put a partition up at the back with a sliding door, which was made into a bedroom. This became Jim's room, as he had been sharing with Phil, it had two single beds in it, and a fitted wardrobe, so we started hosting French students, one boy at a time, who shared with Jim. The cloakroom was situated behind it, so they had their own en suite too.

Carol's earliest
photograph; aged
3 years, 1947.

Carol's mum and dad.
Herne Bay, 1948.

Mum with Carol and
Ron, Herne Bay,
1948.

On the Isle of Wight in 1951.
Carol with her leg in plaster being swung by her mum above,
and her brother Ron sits with
them in the photograph below.

Carol in the Isle of Wight Fancy Dress Competition, 1951.

Carol with brother Ron, 1958.

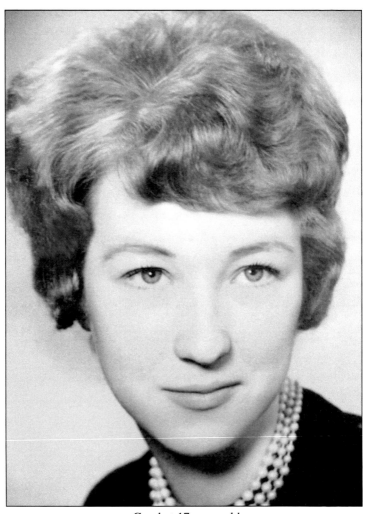

Carol at 17 years old.

Carol's wedding to Mick in September, 1963.
From left: Sylvia, Mick, Carol and Yvonne.

Paula, Carol and Jean
on Carol's 21st birthday party.

Jim's christening in 1966.
Mick's parents Sybil and George standing to the left,
and Carol's mum holding baby Jim next to Carol's dad.

Carol, her mum and baby Jim,
with Tina the dog, Herne Bay, 1966.

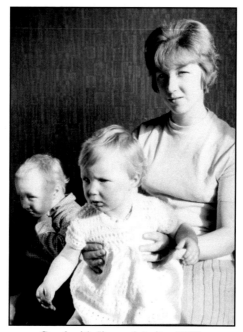

Carol with Jim and Anita, 1968.

Jim holding baby Phil next to Anita, 1971.

Carol and John in Italy, 1984.

Andrea as May Queen, 1985.

We put a big banner across the window with CLOSING DOWN HALF PRICE SALE. Everyone loves a bargain so the customers came in their hordes, and we had a few laughs when they asked to buy things that were not in the sale. John remarked that they even wanted the shirt off his back.

I felt sad that we were losing our business, but we had our family to support so there was no time for sentiment. The sale lasted for six months, and when we were left with just odds and ends, I advertised the last few bits in the local paper, and a lady came round and took the lot for her own shop.

We were now left with an empty shop and disappointed customers, but we couldn't keep going, so we advertised the shop to let, and were inundated with people wanting to rent it. In the end we chose a young couple who had set up their own sunbed business. It was very fashionable at that time, and they were delighted to have their own premises.

During 1979 Anita, who was now eleven, and Andrea, who was now four, joined the local May Queen and attendants. It was a chance for them to indulge in the fun of dressing up; wearing medieval costume, which was a pale blue taffeta dress with a cape. In time, if they took part every year, they would work their way up to being Queen. The pageantry took place on a float all around the local area, and the Queen was always crowned in April, at the start of the season.

In September 1979, at the age of four and a half, Andrea started at Gates Green Road School. Her teacher at nursery had said she was more than ready, because with a bright and enquiring mind, nursery wasn't challenging enough for her. I wrote to the headmaster explaining this, and he found her a place. On her first day, memories came flooding back to me; I had been so happy at that school all those years ago, but of course none of the original teachers were now there. She made new friends; one in particular was a little golden haired girl called Becky Ross, and through their friendship, we got to know her parents, Carole and Nick, who became lifelong friends.

It was now 1980 and I wanted a part time job, which I felt I could fit around the children, although I had no idea what would happen in the holidays. There were not holiday clubs and activities like

d

there are now; but I have always taken each day as it comes, and not looked too far ahead, so I would cross that bridge when I came to it.

There was just one job advertised in the local paper; three and a half days at a china and glass shop in West Wickham, which was just a mile or so up the road. But I didn't even consider it; me working amongst breakable items, I thought not!

But John had spotted it too, and he thought it would suit me nicely.

"No, I couldn't work there, I might break something," was my response.

"You'll get the job when they know you've been running your own shop," he said confidently.

"Yes, but the shop has closed," I said doubtfully.

"We can't help a recession; all the other shops in our parade are suffering," he reminded me.

And it was true, even Dan in the off-licence was grumbling that nobody was buying any drink and they had all given up smoking, he said nobody could afford to have a good time any more. The Italian restaurant where my mum had taken us two years previously had now closed down, and right now that shop was empty.

So I went for the interview, and I got the job. The manager was a very nice man called Liam Phillips, he was the cousin of the owners, and he always treated me with great respect. The shop was double fronted, one side was the lighting department with Lyn and Angela in there. I worked in the china and glass department with Eileen and Pauline, both older ladies. Eileen always looked like she was the manager; she was always smartly dressed, with her hair in a bun, and her stiletto heels clicked as she walked along. Eileen became a close friend for many years, and her husband Alan, who John always got along very well with.

I was so relieved to get the job, and went home very happy; now our finances were on the up. On my first day I arrived full of enthusiasm and very anxious to please. I knew that after being my own boss for quite a few years I would have to learn to take orders, but the end result would be worth it.

I had been there for a few weeks, before I was taken into the lighting department, and several very ornate crystal chandeliers were pointed out to me. I gazed up to admire their beauty, and

74

suddenly I felt like I was going to faint. Panic swept through me. This job was so important to me, I couldn't be fainting just because I was admiring lights! Pauline had noticed my face become pale so she took me back to my own department. I felt disorientated, I had never fainted in my life before. She sat me on a chair in the stockroom, and got me a glass of water to sip.

"You should never look up at the lights, that is why you felt faint," she explained.

I felt a bit stupid, I had started this new job very anxious to please, and show what I could do, not to be sitting in the stockroom after being affected by lights. I thanked her for her kindness, and returned to the shop floor, picking up a duster intending to get busy dusting some of the crystal on display, but Liam had other ideas.

"We are not very busy this afternoon Carol, why don't you go early, and then you will feel better when you come in tomorrow."

This was the last thing I wanted to do; going home sick was not a way of proving myself. However they all agreed, so I had no choice but to go. I got home before John. My friend Audrey met Andrea from school and then Phil off his minibus each day, and then took care of them until John got in, but tonight it was me who took over.

John was surprised to see me home early, so I explained what had happened that day. When the children came in from school, he asked Jimmy and Anita to help prepare the dinner, as "Mum needs a rest." They dutifully peeled potatoes and vegetables, and we spent time organising dinner together. I felt fine for the rest of the evening, which was a relief, and I decided it must have been the lights that had affected me.

I returned to work the next day, which was Saturday, and felt fine, so I put my fainting worries behind me. I was beginning to know the stock now and I enjoyed serving the customers. When I arrived home later Jim and Anita had prepared tea, and the children were all eating it in the kitchen whilst listening to the radio. They were all happy, so I sat in the lounge with John having a welcome cup of tea, and told him about my day.

John was talking to me, saying how glad he was I had the job, and suddenly without warning, I felt a shudder of fear pass through me. I tried to take a deep breath and ignore it, but I couldn't breathe. I felt as if I was in a deep sea sinking, even dying, some strange force seemed to have taken over my whole body. I could hear John from a distance asking me what was wrong. It was like one of those awful dreams, when no matter how hard you try to do something, or get somewhere, your legs are fixed, and you can't.

I gasped, "Help! I'm dying!" and then I must have passed out because when I woke up again, I was in our bed, John was holding my hand with concern written all over his face, and dear Audrey was there too. I remember hearing him say. "A stroke! No Carol, not you, it can't be!"

Audrey was more sensible. "I am sure it isn't; she's only thirty-six, but the doctor will know when he comes."

I still thought I was dying. I could hear them talking about me; breathing was hard, and the main thought in my mind was what would happen to my children, especially Phil, if I died. But when the doctor did arrive, our kindly family doctor, he explained that I was very close to having a nervous breakdown. The panic attacks were caused by my mind taking over my body and not letting me cope.

"You have a lot to deal with, my dear; constant anxiety over Philip, a big family to take care of, and you work as well."

"I have to work; we need the money."

"I am sure you do, and I am not suggesting you give it up, but stress builds up inside and causes the panic attacks."

"Well what can I do then?" I felt so desperate; I needed this job so much. It seemed cruel to me that, after managing to get our finances back on track, I should then be plagued by this.

So the doctor gave me some pills to take, and instructed me to make sure I did get proper rest. He said he thought my job would be good for me as it gave me another focus outside the home. I knew what he meant, it would stop me sitting down and worrying about Phil's future.

That should have been the end of it, but it wasn't. I have never been a person who takes pills, but these pills made me feel a bit detached, and it helped. Although I only took a very low dose, I began to rely on them, which wasn't the answer. The panic attacks continued, but I had to be the master of them; so in the end I learned to say to myself when they came on, "I am only going to faint, not die, so what, I don't care!"

During that period of time I can't have been easy to live with.

My mind played such vile tricks on my body, and I seriously did think I was going mad. Anyone who has suffered in this way, reading this, will know exactly what I mean.

I became convinced that my left arm would not stop shaking, and I couldn't seem to keep it still. My doctor couldn't see that anything was wrong. Then it was the right arm, which I thought was paralysed, so back I went again, and once again I was told it was all right.

Then my neck felt as though someone was choking me. He tested my thyroid gland to see if it was working properly, and it was. Then the most difficult thing of all happened, I developed agoraphobia. If I was in a crowded room, I found I suddenly had to leave because I needed to be alone. I also became scared of leaving the house. I didn't understand what was happening to me, and I could not keep going back to the doctor to be told that nothing was wrong.

Finally it all came to a head one day. First I fainted in the local supermarket and had to be brought home. And then I was in Bromley with Anita and Andrea doing some Christmas shopping, and I felt faint in the clothes store. The kind assistant sat me on a chair outside and stayed with me whilst Anita telephoned for John to come and get me.

When he arrived, he was not impressed. My strange behaviour had been going on for some few months now, and it affected the whole family.

"I can't keep running round after you every time you do this. The doctor told you nothing is wrong," he said curtly.

I sobbed; how cruel was that remark and his lack of understanding hurt me. Did he honestly think I wanted to be like this?

"We're going back to the doctor. Let's find out what's going on."

So accompanied by John, we went again, and my doctor explained why I was having such a hard time mentally.

"You have four children, which would be more than enough for some people, you also have a lot of stress in caring for Philip, plus a broken marriage. It's a wonder you have coped for as long as you have."

This all made sense to me. I was always under stress, but on the surface nobody knew, as I always tried to be positive and to hide my fears, as I didn't want it to affect my children. Had stifling my emotions caused me to be ill like this? Because undoubtedly I was suffering from mental illness. I am not ashamed to admit this; nowadays we are encouraged to say if we are not coping, and to share our worries and fears with others, but in 1980 mental illness wasn't spoken about much; it was swept under the carpet.

So my medication was increased, but that didn't help; it was suppressing my fears and anxiety; I felt like a zombie, and I realised the only way to beat this illness was to stand up to it. John's patience was stretched to the limit, and I felt my family was falling apart.

The one thing I had been determined about was that I wouldn't lose my job. We needed the money, and fate had been so cruel knocking me down at the time when I felt we were getting back on our feet financially. I made mistakes, hid my panic attacks, and pretended all was well. If anyone did notice at the shop, they were tactful, as nothing was said. This lasted for a year; but I fought my demons, they were not going to win, and gradually the panic attacks became less.

My kindly doctor arranged for me to have a home help to look after Phil and Andrea after school until John came in on the days I worked, which meant Audrey didn't have to, so it gave her some free time back; but what a loyal friend she had been to me. Also he arranged for Phil to go into a local children's hospital in West Wickham called Cheyne for the weekends about once a month, and this meant we could spend more time with our other children. When I look back now I am so glad John was tough with me, tough love often gets better results than sympathy, and he did it for all the right reasons.

In the December of 1980 I felt like I was getting my life back on track. I was a lucky woman; I had the love of my husband and my family, and knowing that helped me a lot.

Also in that very same year, after a battle against lung disease that saw her go in and out of hospital for many years, John's mother, Betty Creasey, died. She was found at home, having passed away in her sleep, which quite shook us all up as we were always in regular contact with her. Her life had been snuffed out in an instant, but I still had mine to live.

Chapter Ten

In 1981, Anita, who was thirteen, was showing great promise as a swimmer, and was now competing at County and Southern level. Andrea was only six years old, but she revered her sister and wanted to be just like her. She had learned to swim at three, and by the time she was six, she had joined Beckenham Swimming Club too, and had gone straight into a competitive group. She was at that time quite small for her age, and she was with nine year old children. When the instructor was addressing the group, they used to put her up on another swimmer's shoulders, otherwise she couldn't see or hear what was said. She was referred to as 'The water baby'.

Now that the shop was let out, and I was working at Crest China, it had lost its magic. Then our tenants gave notice, which meant that we would have to find more tenants. For a while we had been thinking it would be nice to buy our own house, and I was particularly keen to buy one on the Coney Hall estate, where I had started my life.

So with the shop as vacant possession, we put the whole building on the market, but were not sure what to expect. To our delight it sold immediately, and was turned into an estate agents. We made enough profit to put towards a house, although we were going to have to have an extension and add extra bedrooms to make it big enough for us. We found a builder and submitted plans, which were duly accepted.

The house was in Birch Tree Avenue, and living further up the road was Carole and Nick. We frequently got together for dinner dates at each other's houses. Carole had been such a good friend to me during my panic attack period. I had run to her house a few times saying I was dying, and she had calmed me down, but she must have wondered what on earth was wrong with me.

The builder let us down at the last minute by raising his price by five thousand pounds. We couldn't borrow any more money, so John vowed he would build the extension himself. And he did just that. With help from his brother Malcolm, they turned a two bedroomed house into a five bedroomed house, and we had a bigger dining room and lounge. The council came along at all stages to pass it, and when it was finished, I felt very proud of their efforts. Malcolm and his girlfriend Linda came over quite frequently on Sundays; they brought the joint, and I cooked dinner for all of us.

Later that year John's decree absolute finally came through. His wife had now found herself a new partner, and had agreed to divorce him. I knew without a doubt that I would be proud to be his wife; he was the love of my life, but I didn't say anything, and he didn't mention it either. I thought regretfully that it might never happen; once bitten, twice shy!

I had settled in well at work and I really enjoyed my job; it was certainly escapism. Whilst I was there, my mind was completely focused on making as many sales as possible. We sold high class china such as Royal Doulton, Aynsley and Wedgwood; bone china fit to grace the most elegant of tables. Then there was Waterford Crystal, Dartington, and the beautiful Royal Doulton figurines, just to name a few of the delightful items we stocked. I learned to appreciate the beauty of English China, and to this day I still have some of it in my house.

Contrary to what I had imagined when I started, I had very few breakages during my time there. I met many customers, and made new friends. It was a challenge to satisfy some of them, but I realised that when I did, it gave me huge job satisfaction. The company used to arrange dinners and get togethers at Christmas, and when I look back now, those years I spent at Crest China, were some of the best in my life.

The thing that amazed me most of all about John was his willingness to share my turbulent life. There was always drama in our house. Phil was in and out of hospital with asthma attacks frequently, one illness followed another, sometimes he couldn't go to school; but it was John who took the day of to be with him if that happened, as he was allowed to book annual leave whenever he wanted to, whereas I couldn't just leave the shop short of staff at the last minute. I had kept my son's difficulties a secret from the management, as I wanted them to think I was reliable, although my friends did know.

In 1981, on 29th July, Charles, Prince of Wales married Lady Diana Spencer, and everyone admired his beautiful young bride, who was only twenty years old. He was thirty-two. I watched the wedding on TV like so many others, so much pomp and ceremony; nobody does it better than Britain.

In 1982 John asked me to marry him, it was quite out of the blue. I had no warning that he would, and maybe I should have played hard to get, but it was my dearest wish to legally be Mrs Carol Creasey, so I happily accepted.

Normally when you marry, you have a gathering for all your friends, but in our case, we had already pretended to be married because I didn't want anyone to know we were only living together. Jim and Anita knew we were not married, but Andrea did not. She was seven years old now, and I was so relieved that our marriage would legitimise her.

I had confided in Audrey, she knew, and was delighted to hear the news. We were going to be married at Bromley Registry Office, and we chose 17th March, which is St Patrick's Day. It was my half day from the shop, and I hugged myself secretly in the morning, as they didn't know I was going to spend my afternoon off getting married!

Audrey and her boyfriend Brian were going to be my witnesses. My dad drove up from Herne Bay; he now had a great relationship with John. Betty and Ron stayed at home as her elderly father was now living with them and he needed someone with him at all times.

It was one of the happiest days of my life, up there with the births of my children. I wore a cream suit with brown accessories, and although it was only March, the sun shone brightly. We went into some gardens afterwards for Brian to take the photos.

But we were never to see those photos, which saddened me. The day after our wedding, Audrey and Brian, who had always had a very volatile relationship, broke up. And to spite her, he refused to have the photos developed. It didn't spite her it was us, we were hoping to have a reminder of a very happy occasion, but the day was over now and we couldn't bring it back. Although I don't have any photos of our wedding day, I have a lot of happy memories stored inside me, which no one can take away.

When I went into work the next day, it felt right; I was now married to my partner just like everyone else. Times have changed so much now, and nobody cares about such things any more.

In 1982 Jim left school. He had benefited from being in a school with smaller classes. His teacher took a great interest in him, and said he worked hard and was an able boy. It was suggested that he went to SELTEC, a local college, for a year, as the further education would benefit him. He used to ride his bike over there every day until it was stolen one day, and then he went by bus. His extra year of study did help him, and he was offered an apprenticeship at a local silk screen printers, so he was able to go straight into a job. The wife of the owner worked at Crest with me, and she told me how hard he worked, and eventually he became a printer.

On 21st June 1982, Princess Diana gave birth to her first son, who was named William, and she gave us a glimpse of her new son when she left the hospital, with a proud and beaming Prince Charles beside her.

It was now 1983, Andrea was eight, and competing and winning swimming galas in the under eleven age group. We travelled all over the place to watch and support her. John more than me, because sometimes with Phil it was difficult. He was twelve now; nearly a teenager, but only in age, not mentally, and his behavioural problems started. He used to get frustrated and have meltdowns in public, and he started biting people. Most of his biting was confined to us, and he also used to bite himself on his arm, which was very distressing. At times life felt like hell to me. I think probably hormonal changes that were happening to him may have caused all this, but it was one of the most testing times for me, and my patience was stretched to the limit on many occasions.

John was a huge support for me. He loved Phil, he had admitted it was impossible not to love him, but he was strict with him, as he really could get through to him. He made him understand his behaviour was not acceptable, and just once he slapped him, and on that occasion he had to because Phil bit me very hard in public and he wouldn't let go; so John had to do something to bring him back to his senses.

I really don't think I would have got through those difficult times without John's strength.

When Phil suddenly stopped eating, our meal table became a battlefield. Every day he would sit there refusing to eat. We didn't know what was wrong, as until then he had always had a good appetite. I took him to the doctor; he looked very frail, his thin little body and stick-like arms and legs looked like they would break. The doctor suggested I gave him a tonic, and if that didn't stimulate his appetite he would have to go into hospital and be fed by a tube, as he was by now anorexic.

When I told John he said he would make sure Phil ate that night. But when we sat down for dinner, it was the same, Phil roared with anger, pushed his plate away, and the girls burst into tears. John sent us out of the room, and I fully trusted him, I knew whatever he did for Phil would be for his own good because underneath his bossy exterior, he really cared.

A few minutes later he called us back in. Phil had eaten a few mouthfuls at last. John explained that he had to hold his nose to stop him spitting his food out, and once Phil got the taste of it, he ate it. He admitted that it hadn't been a pretty sight.

Later that evening, when I was helping Phil get ready for bed, I noticed that his private parts were red and swollen. When the doctor saw it, he immediately put him on antibiotics, as he had a very unpleasant water infection. I thought that this explained his unwillingness to eat, as passing urine would be very painful, and he probably associated eating food with pain but couldn't tell us, which is sad. When a child is ill, and they can't communicate, it must be very distressing for them.

But the crisis passed, Phil's infection healed up, and he started eating properly again. I heaved a sigh of relief, and thanked God for this man who was beside me all the way in trying to help Phil.

Chapter Eleven

Being a parent has to be one of the hardest jobs in the world, trying to get things right and not make mistakes, but being a step-parent is even harder. Disgruntled people who have lost their partner sometimes influence their children against their ex-partner's new love. It is easier to lay the blame on someone else when a marriage fails, and it makes them feel better about themselves.

I failed miserably as a stepmother. I was always sad about this, but John's daughters made it clear that they didn't want to form a relationship with me. For a while he visited them at their home and took them out socially, but then he said they must come to us. I think he wanted them to accept us as a couple, but it never worked.

We all went swimming together on a Saturday, as I worked every other Saturday at the shop, and Phil was at Cheyne. They got on very well with Jim, Anita, and Andrea, who was, of course, their half sister, but all my attempts to be friendly fell on stony ground.

John appeared not to notice their unfriendliness; it was difficult for him being stuck in the middle, so I also pretended not to notice. In their eyes, I was the woman who prevented their dad from coming back to their mum after an argument that had resulted in him moving out and going to live with his mum. If I did break up his family, I am truly sorry, it was never my intention, we just became close friends and then we fell in love.

When we first became a couple, Jim and Anita called him

uncle John, but it wasn't very long before they were asking if they could call him dad. Anita explained: "We want to be a family with a dad, not an uncle; our real dad will always be daddy, that won't change."

John was thrilled to be addressed in this way. He really took his duties as a father and stepfather very seriously. Deep in his heart, obviously Andrea was always his favourite, and when she was a little girl, right up until she was about fourteen, they were so close. She looked like a female version of him, and she had very similar personality traits. I still see them in her to this day. She has always had his kindness and compassion for those worse off than herself.

When you are a step-parent, you can deal with it in two ways. Firstly by being passive, and allowing the parent of the child to do all the correcting and guiding, or you can become involved as if you are their true blood parent, and support your partner through the difficult times. For somebody as strong minded as John, there was no way he was going to sit back and leave everything to me, and I was grateful for his strength and support, as without it I would have not coped at all.

Whilst the children were young it was fine. They respected him so much, and I was glad he was strict with them, as they grew up with manners and the ability to get on with other people. He always tried not to spoil Andrea, but she did sometimes have things that the others didn't have, such as a new swimming costume; whereas Anita might have used her pocket money to buy her own.

But when they all hit their teens, it became much harder. They all rebelled a little, which is only natural, I had expected it. I remembered when I was a teenager, I had gone through a phase thinking that my mother was old fashioned and out of touch with the real world, but nothing could have been further from the truth. I was cheeky to her once because she wouldn't let me go on a midnight walk with some of my friends. I couldn't see anything wrong with it, but now I am viewing it from an adult perspective, I can see exactly why she was having none of it.

Anita was dedicated to her sporting life. As well as being a great swimmer, she had found she also had a talent for running, so she joined Bromley Ladies, and eventually became part of a relay team that broke the British record. She did so well because she was single-minded, the only boys in her life were friends, as she didn't want to be distracted from being a good athlete.

John was not particularly domesticated himself, but he was good at directing, and he made sure the children did their bit to help me. On one occasion he gave Anita the job of peeling the potatoes for me before she went training. But Anita didn't think that was fair, and during an argument she said to him:

"You are not my father; you can't tell me what to do!"

I felt really upset when I heard that. For years she had happily accepted his role in her life, and now she was rejecting him, and being rude. John didn't say if it had upset him, but over a period of time they frequently argued, and she rebelled. I was stuck in the middle; upset for him, and also with her. If she didn't peel the potatoes, it would fall to Jim, who already did a lot to help me as he didn't belong to any club at that time. Her argument was that none of her friends had to do it, so why should she? When I look back now, it was such a petty thing to argue about.

It was only a few days after one of their arguments that she announced that she was going to a party over in Essex that one of her friends was having. She was getting a lift with someone, and she had always been a sensible girl, so we didn't worry too much about her. Anita was always very bubbly and funny, which made her popular, but she didn't drink. She wanted to be the best so she very carefully looked after her health.

We found out later that all her friends had too much to drink, and so were planning to stay the night. Anita was bored with this, she just wanted to come home, so she rang Mick to ask him if he would come and pick her up. But he was not impressed; it was gone midnight, and he didn't want to turn out at that time of night.

So she rang me in tears saying all she wanted to do was come home. John heard some of the conversation, and asked what was wrong. When I told him he came on the phone to ask for the address, and said he was going to get her. I was amazed; she had not dared to ask him, because at that time they were not on the best of terms, but it made no difference to him, he went and brought her safely home. They didn't get home until about two o'clock, and I didn't like to go to bed, so I waited until they returned. She thanked him and then went off to bed, and we all slept a bit later the next morning.

So life continued to be challenging for us, and when we

reached 1984, several things happened that year that stand out to me. Firstly I became forty, not the sort of age one can forget, and in celebration of that, John had arranged for Malcolm and Linda to come and stay at our house and look after the children, as we were having our first holiday without them. Phil was being looked after at Bucket and Spades, an organisation at Hastings that offered respite care to families who had a child with special needs.

We couldn't afford anything more than a holiday by coach, and I remember having a stiff back and legs when we got there, after travelling for thirty hours. It soon wore off, and our companions on the coach were great company. Whilst we were travelling, the coach guide told us about an optional excursion we could go on when we got there, and finished off by saying:

"By the way, it is a four hour coach journey!" to which one of our new friends remarked:

"Well, after this, we should manage it standing on our heads."

We, of course, all erupted into laughter.

We went to Italy. It was a wonderful carefree holiday; we visited Venice, went on a gondola, and enjoyed all the delights that Italy could offer. We came back rested and fit, only to find that Jim had been knocked off his bike on the way to college and had to go to hospital. Luckily he was OK.

One Sunday we were having dinner, the radio was on, and some very lively music was playing. Phil loved the music, he rose from his chair, and leaned over to help clear the plates, and suddenly I noticed his arms twitching; he couldn't seem to pick up the plates. He tried again, and then his face became contorted, his body stiffened, and he crashed to the ground, dragging the tablecloth and all the contents with him. He then lay on the ground twitching, and I realised with horror that my son was having an epileptic fit.

We called the doctor, who came round immediately, but by then Phil was conscious but looking a little dazed. The doctor explained that he probably had a headache now. He didn't seem surprised about the fit, and warned us that the fits might be a regular occurrence, not to panic when it happened, and not to put our fingers in his mouth, as when a patient is fitting, they could bite very hard. I felt devastated for Phil; didn't he have enough to cope with?

Andrea, who was now nine years old, came home from school one day with a sad story. Her friend Katy at school had a neighbour who organised dog rescue. She had a beautiful collie retriever cross; he was six months old, and they urgently needed to find a home for him. My first reaction was no, I had vowed after losing Tina, never to have a dog again. Not only that, I felt I had enough to cope with, but I could tell that John was keen, and so was Andrea.

Then the lady asked if she could just bring him round for half an hour, just to see if we liked him. When he arrived, John tied him to a long piece of rope, then took him in the garden and played with him for about two hours. He had been ill treated by his last owners, and John was trying to gain his confidence.

I stayed in the kitchen, trying not to get involved and feeling a bit as if nobody cared about my opinion. But when John brought him inside, I could not avoid looking at him. He cocked his head on one side, then sidled up to me with his tail wagging, and I was instantly smitten.

Suddenly all the negative thoughts I had been thinking, such as dog hairs, muddy paws, and all the extra responsibility having a dog entailed, faded away. He was gorgeous, and he became a very faithful friend and family pet.

John was his primary carer, and Prince adored his master. I think it was his first meeting in the garden that cemented his faith and trust in human beings again after it had been cruelly shattered. Anita also took him with her when she was training; they jogged all around the area. I walked him when I had time, but it was mostly with John and Andrea, when we went out as a family if the others were with their dad. He really did enrich our lives. We took more exercise, and he loved to play piggy in the middle, jumping up to try and get the ball when we were tossing it back and forth. Prince had the most wonderful nature and he was a great family dog; he loved us all, but he followed John around a lot, and there was a special relationship between them.

During that same year, Anita was doing coursework for her GCSEs as the exams were now called. She was doing English, and she asked me for some guidelines about how to write a decent essay, and also to double check her spellings. I have always loved spelling, and pride myself on not making many mistakes. When I looked through the papers that she showed me, I felt shame go through me. I had always been good at English, but because my head was all over the place at the time, I had failed English at school. These papers looked easy, and just because I was forty, that didn't mean I was past it. Mum wasn't here to be proud of me if I passed, but Dad was.

So I enrolled at evening classes on a Wednesday evening every week. I diligently did my homework, because when you are paying for something, then you are not going to waste the money. When the course was over I took the exam, and passed grade B. This spurred me on to achieve more; so during the next few years I studied and passed, all with grade B, English Literature, Social and Economic History, Psychology, Sociology, and then finished off with English Literature Advanced Level. It was during those classes, when we had to write essays about books we were studying, that my teacher asked me if I realised that I had a flair for writing. She liked my essays. My dad was now thrilled that I had seven O-level passes and one A-level, so if any of you out there think it's too late after you leave school to study and take exams, take heart from me. It made no difference to my job, but it made me feel better about my wasted last year at school!

I am pleased to say that, after a bit of guidance from me, Anita too passed her English Language, and with the rest of her results being good enough, applied for a job in Lloyds bank. She was going to start as a junior and work her way up, and I knew she would, she had both talent and ambition. Jobs at this time were sparse, so some students went on to sixth form and university in the hopes that more qualifications would give them more choice for a job, but Anita knew what she wanted, and she got the job. It also meant that she could carry on with her running and competing, as she didn't work on Saturdays.

This was the year that John had finished paying the mortgage off on the home he had shared with his first wife, so that immediately meant he had more money. We stopped doing the pools rounds, and I used to look forward to evenings in at the end of the day. With the extra money he now had, John bought me a dishwasher, microwave, new washing machine and cooker, as well as fitting a new kitchen. They may not sound very romantic presents, but it was to make my life easier, and it certainly did. The one thing that did amuse us was, previously the children had argued about who should wash the dishes, now they were arguing about whose turn it was to fill and empty the dishwasher. In the end Jim decided it was his job, and to this day, when he comes to stay with me, he still does it.

By the end of 1984, I had been at Crest China for four years, Liam had now become one of the directors, and we had had a succession of managers. The company believed training up young people for the job was the answer, but sometimes they didn't prove to be responsible enough. Eileen had now retired and gone to live in Devon, so we didn't see her and Alan that often now.

My job meant a lot to me, I knew the stock, and I prided myself on remembering a lot of the customers' names. We did a lot of local trade, and often if somebody ordered a dinner service, or something heavy, I would deliver it personally to them on the way home. I also got on well with the girls I worked with, and gradually I had managed to fight off the threat of a breakdown. I had thrown away the pills, and faced all my fears head on. During my life since, if I ever feel a bit panicky, and it can happen, I make myself slow down, because that vulnerability is always there, and it's up to me to make sure it never overcomes me again.

In fact the job was very good for me, it gave me something else to focus on outside my family. The company were strict but fair; we were not allowed to sit down, so there were no chairs on the shop floor, and the door was kept open, no matter how bad the weather, to encourage customers to come in. We were not allowed to wear trousers, and later there became a uniform of a navy skirt and a white blouse, which I did like wearing, it made me feel more professional.

During one of the periods when Phil was in hospital, one of the doctors suggested that they gave us a nebuliser to keep at home so he didn't have to keep coming in every time he had an asthma attack. Previously we had not been allowed one because of the cost, but in the end it saved them much more money, because we were able to control his asthma at home. So that was another hurdle we had climbed over. Phil has never got the hang of using an inhaler, so the nebuliser has always been a part of his life. It is a small machine with a face mask, and it puffs out Ventolin, which helps to keep his airways open. This replaced oxygen tents, which hospitals had years ago.

Jim was now eighteen, and he did a part time job at the local pub. Guess what, he was collecting glasses and loading and unloading the dishwasher. One of the girls he worked with had organised a collection for him, and we were secretly invited to the presentation. We had no idea what the present was, so were as surprised as he was when a brand new bike was wheeled in for him. They had heard about his other one being stolen, so it was a very thoughtful gift. Looking around at all the faces there made me realise just how kind people are at times.

By the end of 1984, Anita already had promotion at work; she was no longer the junior, so her wages went up accordingly. Her running career was going well, and she had, in fact, taken part in Lloyds Bank sports events, and done very well there.

But my life was about to change again in the following year, and decisions would need to be made. I had to make sure that any decision I made would be the right one, or else live to regret it. Not that I believe in regrets; we can't change what is done, we just have to make the best of it.

On 15th September 1984, Princess Diana's second son, and last child, was born. He was named Prince Harry. Great Britain celebrated, along with Charles and Diana.

Chapter Twelve

So 1985 arrived, and Andrea had now been taking part in the May Queen celebrations for six years. It was very exciting for her, as this year she was to be Queen. She had tried her dress and crown on, and it looked lovely, and I was all set to go with John to see her crowned.

But we hadn't reckoned on the weather; it might have been April, but mother nature didn't smile down on us. Just before we left home, it started to snow, big heavy snowflakes came down. I put on my warmest coat, and now I was worried how Andrea would stay warm. The dress was not thick, and they only wore a little cape over it. But of course children don't notice the cold like adults, and they all stood there, faces glowing whilst snow flakes were falling around them, and Andrea was duly crowned.

One day Liam came over from head office. We had just lost another manager, and I guessed he had come over to sort out something. His words took me completely by surprise.

"Carol, you have been here for five years. You know the job inside out, how would you like to be manager?"

I was amazed, I got on quietly with my job, and I didn't think anyone noticed me. Being a manager would mean interviewing staff and running the shop. I was by nature a shy person, who preferred just to be in the background but, on the other hand, I felt it was an honour to be asked.

"It will, of course, mean you working five days a week, and every Saturday, but you can choose what day off you would like."

"Thank you for asking me Liam, I will have to go home and consult with my family, it's only right."

"Of course, you can let me know tomorrow. Several people have applied, but we don't think any of them are suitable."

After he had gone, I thought about his words. I wondered who had applied; it was more than likely someone within the company. I worked with four others at our West Wickham branch; it could be one of them, so I said nothing to anyone.

I thought about it all day, and before I even went home, had decided that it wouldn't work. It was true that Phil was often at Cheyne at the weekend, but how could I work every Saturday and leave everything to John? Then there was Phil; working for three and a half days had worked out, although now we opened all day on a Wednesday, so one week I worked three, the next it was four, but that extra day made me full time, and sometimes he was ill and couldn't go to school. I couldn't let the responsibility of looking after him if he was ill be dumped on John alone. Then there was school holidays, so many of them. No, it was impossible, I had to put my family first.

But when I shared it with the family, they were very impressed, and thought I should take it.

"If it won't be too tiring for you, I think it's a great idea, and I am very proud of you!" said John.

The others agreed.

"But look at all the things that could go wrong," I reminded them.

"No, don't do that. Haven't we always taken each day as it comes? If it becomes too difficult then we will have to think again, but it's a great opportunity for you, and it's obvious your company have faith in you, and think of the extra money you will earn."

I had forgotten that part of it; I would actually be able to afford to send Phil to a holiday club for disabled children which had recently been set up. It may have been a funny time in my life to have an ambition to pursue a career in management, but it was the only time it had been possible, so with the blessing of my family, I intended to embrace it.

I telephoned Liam at head office the next day, and he was delighted that I was taking the job. He then explained I would be going on a Royal Doulton course, which meant I would be away from home for two days. I hadn't expected that, and it was during the week when Phil was at home, so I wondered how they would cope at home.

But I needn't have worried, everything went very smoothly at home thanks to a concerted family effort. I am lucky that I have a close bond with my family, and they have never let me down.

I stayed at a very classy hotel, courtesy of Crest China. I travelled to Stoke-on-Trent by train, and was met at the station by a taxi, which took me there. The two days I spent there were filled with activities. First we went to the factory to see the glass being blown, and admired the finished product. Then there was a trip to the potteries to watch the china being formed on the potter's wheel. We were given leaflets about the products; what they were made of, how to care for them, and much more. I studied them all carefully, because when you are selling such finely crafted products, it's very important to have knowledge about them. I wanted to do my job properly, and I also wanted my staff to as well.

We were also given very nice meals at the hotel; a cooked breakfast, a tasty lunch, and then a splendid dinner in the evening, served with wine and cocktails if you wanted. I had made friends with a young girl, who was a trainee manager at another company up in London, so we had our dinner together in the evening, and we both commented that staying in this hotel had given us a glimpse of a life we could only dream about, and what a great experience it had been.

John was waiting for me at the station when I got home, and I shared my two days with him. He could see how much I had enjoyed the experience, and I shared it with the others too when I got home. When I returned to work the next day, I had new employees to interview; several women had applied, and I found it was easier than I thought. I selected two, the company policy was always to choose people you felt would stay, and the two I chose stayed as long as I did.

I had little training sessions with the staff during quiet periods in the shop. I wanted them to be equipped with knowledge about the products they were selling. I had learned how to cash up and do the banking, and none of it was as hard as I thought it would be. Knowing this gave me confidence, and I took on the role of always dealing with customer complaints myself. I found that if I sorted out their grievances, they would return again to shop with us, and I enjoyed the challenge, especially if I could tame a disgruntled customer.

The shop had lost its way, with frequent changes of management and part time staff changes, so I was delighted to see the takings going up. Crest China was a company business which had been going for fifty years, and they had branches all over the south east region, the largest being our Bromley branch. But when the figures were collaborated, to my delight, my branch was leading with takings, as although Bromley took more money, they also had more staff and higher overheads. There was no rent to pay for West Wickham, as they owned the premises and the flat above it, so it made a good profit for them. Together with my staff we worked hard to please the customers, and we had many regular ones who returned time and again.

After I had been a manager for about six months, the company opened a new shop at Tunbridge Wells. I was asked if I would go down there for a few days to help get it started. I knew I could trust my staff to look after the shop, so I agreed. Then they put a manager in there, but she wanted to have Wednesdays off, so for a few months I travelled there to run the shop on Wednesdays.

I was not the only ambitious one. John had always wanted to be a BT instructor. It was usually older men that were given the role, and many courses had to be taken and passed before he could qualify. He was forty-two, and most instructors were over fifty, because they often addressed men in their forties who preferred to be instructed by an older person.

But his manager was impressed with John's keenness. He had a great speaking voice, and was always smart and well dressed; he really looked the part, so he started on a course which would eventually lead to giving him the qualifications he needed. As a young man, John looked like the actor Robert Wagner, who had always been a favourite of mine.

Now that I was earning a manager's wage it made quite a difference to us. I was able to put Phil into a holiday club organised for children with special needs. When I collected him one evening, the lady who ran it told me in a rather hushed voice, so no one else could hear, that my son had bitten Sarah, the daughter of the south east Kent psychologist, and the reason why I winced at the news was because I had an appointment with that same lady in a few days. Phil was under her care, but I couldn't help wondering for how much longer after he had taken a lump out of her daughter.

So when I took Phil for the appointment with her a few days later, which I had arranged for a Friday, which was my day off from work, I sat there nervously wondering whether I should apologise for his behaviour, or say nothing in the hopes that she didn't realise who the culprit was.

She was reading through Phil's notes, and I sat there with him; it felt like an elephant was in the room. She looked at me over her glasses, and said, "How does Philip like the holiday play group?"

I wasn't expecting that; so she did know. I blurted out nervously, "He seems to like it, but I know he bit Sarah the other day. . ."

She laughed. "Oh yes, but it was Sarah's own fault, she pulled his hair first, we keep telling her not to pull hair."

I gazed at her in surprise; I hadn't expected her to be so understanding about it, I knew how much Phil's bites could hurt.

"But he shouldn't be biting. He does it to us sometimes, and I know it hurts."

"He will grow out of it you know, won't you Phil?" she smiled at him when she spoke. "Just be patient, not being able to speak makes it so hard for him. Biting is something toddlers go through, and although Philip is fourteen, his mind is not; but it is a phase. Sarah will live. She knew exactly what she had done; she can speak, and she told me all about it."

I looked at her with even more admiration. Such a high powered job she had, and she had a daughter with special needs, but she still found the time to help others. I voiced my thoughts.

"How do you manage to cope with such an important job, and cope with your daughter's special needs? It's amazing!"

"It's no more amazing than your job. You have four children, I just have one. My mother helps out, and my husband and I share duties, as we both work from home a lot."

I didn't think anything I did was amazing; I was just another mum working to help with the family's finances, but lucky enough to be doing a job I loved. Phil was sitting next to me with that familiar faraway look in his eyes that meant he was immersed in his own little world. I knew that he understood what we were saying, and so he had retreated to his place of safety where he could stay and avoid being scolded for his misdemeanours.

After the meeting was over, I took him home, and whilst we were travelling in the car, I spoke very firmly to him.

"Phil, it's not nice to bite people, especially little girls. You mustn't do it!"

When we got out of the car he grabbed my hand and pulled me towards the house. I knew what he wanted, a drink and a snack, and I made him sit down at the table. If I let him get the squash out, he would pour it into a glass and drink it without diluting it, and once he had made himself sick doing this. I got a Kit Kat out of the cupboard, and his face lit up; Phil has always loved chocolate.

By the time his snack was eaten, the rest of the family started to come in, all talking about their days. When John arrived I told him what the psychologist had said about Phil growing out of his biting one day.

"Roll on that day!" said John drily. Phil by then had gone in the other room to watch the TV with the others, so he couldn't hear what was said.

"We will look back on it one day, and say, 'do your remember when Phil used to bite?' "

And John was right, I am looking back now, thankful that it's only a memory.

e

Chapter Thirteen

In 1986 my brother Ron was now forty-nine years old. My dad and Betty had been married for eight years, and Ron lived with them. He couldn't afford to do otherwise because he wasn't very highly paid. He had worked for the council in the parks department, and in a factory that made dolls, but none of these jobs paid very well.

In the local newspaper there was a lonely hearts club, and he was always saying how much he would like a girlfriend, so my dad wrote off on his behalf to try and find someone. He went out with a couple of women, but it didn't last, and then he had a letter from a lady who said she was a widow, with four sons. She was aged about thirty.

So he met up with her and was smitten immediately. It wasn't long before they had decided to get married, and I was so thrilled for Ron. She asked Andrea to be her bridesmaid, which we were all thrilled about, and also asked if she had a friend who would be prepared to be the other one. Her family didn't seem to be involved, so she asked if my dad could give her away, and he was very happy to do this.

The wedding went off very well. Andrea and Donna, her friend from swimming, wore lilac long dresses, and they both looked lovely, they had white shoes, which contrasted well with the outfit, and flowers in their long hair.

So Ron was now married, and had left home to live with his new wife in her council house at Aylesham. I hoped that my mum was looking down and seeing this, she would have been absolutely thrilled to see Ron so happy.

*   *   *   *

I was finding it increasingly harder to cope with Phil. When a two year old throws a tantrum in public, or bites, the situation can be kept under control, even if they throw themselves on the floor in anger. You simply scoop them up and carry them off. But when you have a teenage boy such as Phil, who is as tall as you are, and very strong, with the body of a teenager, but the mind of a toddler, and they have a meltdown, not only is it embarrassing, but it's also frightening, and there is no way you can pick them up and carry them off! Caring for Phil was as much as I could cope with, and sometimes even that was too much. But I had to hold everything together. I had a full time job, a family and a husband, and I didn't want to let them down. I had known it would be a challenge when I became a manager, but the challenge was not at work, it was at home. Oh the teenage years, how they can wear you down! How nice when you can look back on them and realise it's all behind you, and your sanity has remained intact.

Sadly my brother's marriage did not last. He turned up on dad's doorstep one day, and we were all so sorry for him. Dad and Betty knew how much he wanted to come back home, so he moved back in. He also brought his wife's dog with him. It was a Jack Russell; the dog adored Ron, and he always took great care of her and walked her.

But it had a quick temper, and when we visited with the family, it attacked Anita's legs under the table. I think it was frightened of children. So after that we were always careful to keep away from her, and I told the children not to play with her or stroke her. They were used to romping with Prince, but they realised that not all dogs were as laid back as him.

The Jack Russell was not aggressive towards Prince at all; it just seemed to dislike humans, except Ron, and I am sure the trust she had towards him must have meant a lot to him at this difficult time in his life. Betty and Dad had another dog which she also got on with.

A year later, in 1987, Anita announced she wanted to go to Summer Camp in America for three months. In the newspaper they were asking for nineteen year olds upwards to spend three months in the summer holidays, teaching sport to youngsters on holiday. She had enquired at work, and they had agreed to keep her job open whilst she was away.

Because it was only for three months, I thought it was a good idea. Being away, and having to look after herself, would help her to mature. John and I had both found her argumentative during her teens, but that was all, she was far too dedicated to her sport to indulge in some things that other teenagers did; her self-discipline was good. As a young child she had been sunny and happy, and I was confident she would become that person again.

So off she went; and at the time, I hadn't realised how devastated Andrea was to lose her big sister and role model. I missed her, but comforted myself with the thought that she would soon be back.

But fate had other ideas. Anita had been spotted running. Her talent was recognised and she was offered a scholarship. This had been her main reason for going, as sporting scholarships are more readily given in the States than in Britain.

She found herself a job as a nanny to a little girl of eighteen months, and she became very fond of her. But when she wrote to me she commented about the couple she worked for, saying:

"Mum, they sit at each end of a large table when we eat; they don't speak to each other, and there is no love in that house."

I realised she was homesick; maybe she thought we weren't so bad after all. I was missing her a lot now, and all the silly arguments there had been seemed ridiculous. She would have to stay there for three years to complete her scholarship, and I knew I would really miss her.

But it wasn't just the scholarship that was keeping her there. She had met Tom whilst she was out jogging. He was her first serious boyfriend; she had been too pre-occupied with training and running in the past to start a relationship in England. I wasn't sure if it was just like a holiday romance and might not last; only time would tell.

There were no computers then, so the only contact we had with each other was by telephone. We used to take it in turn to ring each other once a week because there were no mobile phones either. She seemed to be her bubbly self again. She had always been an independent girl; out of all my children, she was the one who had less of my attention because she didn't need it, she always knew what she wanted from life. And she looked so much like me at the same age, that I always felt very close to her and shared her values. She also had a great sense of humour and could always make me laugh.

She seemed to be enjoying the way of life in America, and her romance with Tom continued. Apparently he was in the navy, a helicopter pilot, and he would be having two year postings all over the place. So Anita would have periods of time when he was away, but she intended to keep her head down and study with her scholarship.

She came home to see us for a week or so. It was lovely to have her back, but it was only a visit. She paid them a visit at Lloyds Bank and thanked them for holding her job open, but explained she would be away for three years, so regretfully she would have to leave. They all wished her well, understanding that she was young with her whole life ahead of her. It's normal to take those opportunities when they come along, and I understood too, and was very proud of her, but the thought of not having her around for three years was a sobering one. I hid my sadness; I wasn't going to resort to emotional blackmail, but I knew we wouldn't be the same without her around; she was the joker of the family, the one who was fun to be with; we would all miss that.

It was now 1988, and after successfully entering and winning the Kent championships in Individual Medley during 1987, Andrea went a level higher, by competing in the Southern Counties. Her swimming coach was very excited, and spoke about her being in the Esso Youth Squad.

Always an animal lover, she came home from school one day with another sad story. Her friend's cat had given birth to kittens in a shed, the family didn't want the kittens, and they were all going to be drowned if they could not find homes for them.

I wasn't sure if we could bring up a dog and cat together. Prince was now four years old, and a very good tempered dog. Everyone thought that he would not object to a tiny kitten, and I felt a cat would not make much difference to us. John's advice to Andrea, who was allowed to go and choose one, was to get a big tom cat, who would sit on the wall and scare off other cats. She came back with Charley, who was the runt of the litter; so tiny that she always looked like a kitten. When we took her to the vet we were informed that our kitten was a girl, but the name stayed, just spelt differently, because it suited her.

John conceded defeat; and although Charley was tiny, she had the heart of a lion. She was a feisty little girl, half feral, as her father had been an outside cat, but she was strong and healthy. She spent most of the time outside, I tried to domesticate her by buying her a nice fluffy and cosy little bed, but she would have nothing to do with it. In the end I moved it into the garage, and was amused one day to go in there when it was raining, only to find her curled up inside it.

She got on fine with Prince, who treated her with huge respect. When we opened the door in the morning for them to go out, he stood back respectfully, away from the door, whilst she slipped in front and ran outside. If there were any bruisers out in the garden, and sometimes there were, as the local toms had cottoned onto the fact she was so small, even though she had been spayed, Prince would dash out there barking and clear the garden so her ladyship could make her grand exit onto the path.

Another important event in 1988, which was unexpected, was as well as Anita visiting us, Tom came too. There was a special reason for that; he asked John and I for permission to get engaged to Anita. I was struck by his old fashioned respectful attitude; it was charming. It was during that visit that Anita spoke to John, saying how sorry she was that she had been a stroppy teenager, she had seen the error of her ways. I knew then, at the age of twenty, I had finally got my lovely daughter back. John said nothing, but he just gave a wry smile.

Now that she was engaged to Tom, I was beginning to realise that Anita might be living in America even after she had finished her scholarship. It was a sobering thought, and I knew I would miss her, we were so close, but when your child grows up and flies the nest it isn't about how Mum feels. My job was to support whatever decision she made, because we are all entitled to live our own life. If she was happier with Tom in America, I must swallow down my feelings. We had brought her up to be independent, not to live in our pockets, so I should be proud of what she had already achieved. How many girls of nineteen would have travelled to a strange country, alone? I don't think I would have been as mature at her age. And then living with strangers. Anita had always had her head screwed on right. She had drive and ambition, and I was sure she had a very bright future ahead of her.

A date had not yet been set for the wedding, but it was to be a military wedding at the Academy on Long Island, Andrea would be a bridesmaid, as well as Tom's four sisters. I had not been on a plane for years, and didn't like flying, but I knew on this occasion I would have to fight my fears and get on that plane, because there was no way that I would miss this wedding. I could feel excitement building up inside me already, even though they had not decided exactly when it would take place.

Just before the wedding, Jim went over to visit Anita in America. He went with her whilst she tried on her Wedding Dress. With a patience most young men wouldn't possess, he waited whilst she made sure it fitted her right. Obviously she didn't want Tom to see it before the wedding, but once she got the OK from Jim, a man of few words, that it looked great on her, she was happy. I also would love to have been involved, but I knew I had to be content with attending the wedding. I could use part of my annual leave, and I couldn't wait!

Chapter Fourteen

I had been struggling to cope with Phil during his teenage years. Without the strength and commitment from John it would have been a lot harder, but I finally had to admit defeat. I was in contact with Mrs Fry, who was attached to Farnborough hospital. She had been a great help in arranging Phil's stays at Cheyne, but we both knew it wasn't really a suitable placing. Most of the children there were in wheelchairs, with severe disabilities. There was no stimulation for Phil, and he had taken to sitting himself in a wheelchair and ferrying it around, because seeing all of them made him think he should do the same.

The hospital was a small cottage hospital; it was old and needed updating, and it was understaffed, but none of this was the fault of those working there. The most important thing they gave to Phil was love, and so my memories of his time there are grateful memories. They supported me and my family, because when you have a child with special needs, it does affect the whole family.

One day when I was meeting with Mrs Fry I confessed my inability to cope any more. I felt hopeless and helpless, and she was so understanding; before I knew it, my composure slipped, and I was in tears. She looked at me with horror when I confessed what a hopeless mother I was.

Nobody, myself included, wanted me to have a breakdown. I had come so close to it, and spent a couple of years fighting it off, so she made some enquiries. It seemed that the Bromley area had no vacancies anywhere for the needs of Phil. They had recently built a complex of sheltered housing, but Phil needed one to one care for twenty-four hours a day to ensure he never harmed himself. He would never be able to go out into the community unaccompanied, as he had no awareness of danger such as busy roads, and he couldn't speak to explain himself, although he had always been able to understand what is said to him.

Mrs Fry called me in to see her a few days later, and explained that although Bromley had nothing to offer, there was a house at Hastings with a family living there, and room for Phil plus two other autistic young men to go and live with them. He would attend a day centre from Monday to Friday, and be taken out at the weekend for social events. He could come home to stay with us whenever we wanted, but at least once a month. I didn't know what to say; by my own admission I could no longer cope, but I had expected him to be somewhere nearby so I could pop in and see him every day. And my conscience bothered me too. What sort of mother was I to give up on my boy? I was in turmoil, because when you have an angry child, it affects the whole family, and the rest of the family deserved to be considered too.

She saw my reaction, explained that Hastings was the only option, and suggested we paid the family a visit. The plan was they were going to get the house up and running, then carers would take over. Phil would have a one to one carer twenty-four hours a day.

So John and I went to view the house, and so did Mick. We saw the room Phil would have as his bedroom, we met the couple, who were lovely, and slowly I began to accept that it was the best thing for Phil, for me, and for the whole family.

I must confess that the day he went there I had such an ache in my heart, my little boy was going to be so far away; my vulnerable little son. And for a few weeks afterwards I shed a few tears when I went to bed. I hid my anguish from John, Jim and Andrea, as obviously they mattered to me too.

But as the months went by we settled into a routine, and it worked for us all. Phil's epileptic fits were now under control, thanks to Epilim. He was on a dairy free diet to help his eczema, and within days of moving to Hastings, his asthma went away. We still need a nebuliser, but it's used to prevent wheeziness because he can't cope with an inhaler. His health was gradually improving, and so was his temper. Maybe his frustration had been because he didn't feel well, and couldn't say. I can't imagine being in a world where I couldn't speak to people and explain my needs, he has had to cope with that for all of his life.

And he has accepted having two homes. When he is due home, they tell him, and he gets out his bag to pack his clothes. Likewise, at the end of his stays with us, when I say he is going back to Hastings, out comes the bag again, and he starts to pack it. Phil has always been very tidy and organised; he leaves his shoes and slippers in a certain place, and I am careful not to move them.

I have seen over the years, as he has now been there for thirty years, how much the staff there love Phil. He is a charmer, and seems to know how to get the best out of people, and of course he is also incredibly brave. I am very lucky that my son is so well cared for, and will continue to be when I am no longer around. If I had kept him at home, when I passed away it would have been devastating for him.

Going back to 1989, I am pleased to say he emerged from that difficult period a very sunny and happy person. The biting stopped, and also the self harming. Although Phil didn't like being touched, within recent years he has learned to hug, and I still get a lump in my throat when he comes up to us, one by one, and hugs us so tightly with a big smile on his face. It means so much, this clumsy expression of his love.

It's reserved for family only, and he likes to initiate it, so we respect that. I believe that all children thrive on love; Phil certainly has, and he is very dearly loved by everyone.

It was a special year for Andrea. With her swimming in 1989 she competed in the Nationals, and came fourth in the hundred metres breaststroke. She was also part of a medley relay and they won gold, which was a huge boost for Beckenham Swimming Club.

I have a photograph in my lounge which was taken by a professional photographer, it shows Andrea with determination written all over her face, in her breaststroke race. It was such a good photo that it was used on the cover of a swimming magazine.

Another very important event in 1989 was Tom and Anita's wedding. Usually a mother and daughter plan the wedding together, they go out and choose the dress, address the invitations, and work out how many people to invite.

But this was a completely different situation. The wedding was being held in New York State, at the Naval Academy, and it was to be a military wedding, with Tom dressed in his uniform. I was told it was all under control, and all we needed to do was to get on a plane and come. After a lot of thought, Anita had asked Mick to give her away; he was her birth father, and I think he would have been devastated if he was not asked.

John had offered to drive the car that the bride and her dad would travel in. It was a bit awkward obviously, but for Anita's sake, and for mine too, John and Mick needed to treat each other with respect. So he was the chauffeur for them and he carried out his duty meticulously, even driving Anita and Tom after they were married.

We met Tom's parents for the first time, and his brother, and his four sisters, who along with Andrea were bridesmaids. Andrea was only fourteen, but she looked so grown up in her bridesmaid dress. She was the youngest out of all of them, but was so thrilled to be her sister's bridesmaid. Her dress was deep blue, a colour that suits her well.

Anita had her long blonde hair dressed on top of her head, her dress was beautifully styled with a train; she looked absolutely radiant, as brides usually do. It was touching to see the pride in Tom's eyes when he saw her, and we could see they were deeply in love.

The reception was held at a hotel, and we got to know Tom's parents better. His mother was also called Carol, and his father worked for the FBI as an agent. I am never very good in social situations, as I am very shy, but we were all made to feel very welcome.

We were staying at the house of a lady called Chris, who had been like a second mother to Anita whilst she was away from home. Chris was a running coach, and had spotted Anita's talent. She thoroughly approved of Tom, as we did, and said she had known right from the start that they were meant to be together. Those words gave me such a glow, because knowing my daughter was now going to live her life so far away from home, I wanted her to be safe and loved.

Anita and Tom went away to the Bahamas for their

107

honeymoon, and we spent the rest of our time out there sightseeing. I remember going to see the Statue of Liberty on a grey day; the weather was not great that week, but the sun had shone on the wedding day, and that was all that mattered.

It had taken every bit of my courage to get on that plane. I have always had a fear of heights, and can only relax once we are down on the ground again. Unfortunately that fear has never left me, but it hasn't stopped me from making regular trips to see my American family, as I call them.

We took a lot of our own photos, so when I returned to work, I shared them with my staff, who all wanted to hear about the wedding. They all knew Anita because she had often popped into the shop to see me when she lived at home.

Life felt a bit flat for a while after that; there had been so much excitement leading up to the.wedding, and now it was over. But John had now passed all his courses, and was invited to be an instructor. I was so proud of him. He was now forty-six, and had finally achieved his dream. It wasn't just the extra money he earned that thrilled us, it was that after all his hard work, he was doing a job that he loved. Now he went to work in smart suits and not BT overalls. He had his own office and he planned to continue with this job until BT retired him at the age of sixty.

They had not been married very long before Anita rang me to say she was pregnant. Her baby was due in March 1990. I could hardly believe that I was going to be a grandmother. I was going to be forty-six when the baby arrived, but I was thrilled. My little girl was going to be a mum.

We paid a visit to them as soon as we could after the baby was born. Becky entered the world in March 1990; she was a big baby, over nine pounds in weight, but we didn't get to see her straight away.

We visited when Becky was about five months old. She was a beautiful baby, and like mostly everyone in our family, she had blonde hair and blue eyes. Anita and Tom arranged her christening whilst we were staying, and it was a lovely moment with the candles burning in the chapel, to see the priest, by the font, anointing her head with holy water.

I was so happy to be a part of that, but it was a sobering

thought that I would not be on hand to help babysit, or be a part of her life, or that of any brothers or sisters that she might have later, because I was so far away. The best I could do was to visit annually, and that didn't feel enough. I wanted to watch her growing up.

I explained all that to John on the way home, and he understood totally. Squeezing my hand, he said, "We'll make sure you get over as often as it's possible."

Well I only had limited holiday time from work every year, and John and I would want our own holiday, so it could be done, but it wasn't easy. It was such a strong feeling inside me, I almost felt like I had given birth to Becky myself. And it was that feeling, and others, that were propelling me on at the time, and gave John and I a moment of madness, which was to bite us back later.

Chapter Fifteen

Everyone has a dream, and I had come full circle and ended up living at Coney Hall, where I first started my life. But some of the memories I had stored as a child proved to be different when viewed through the eyes of an adult. I had thought the road we lived in was long, but it wasn't. The school playground had become a block of retirement flats, and the rough ground with the old oak trees, that led from Coney Hall up to West Wickham, had now been made into a main road on which you could not park.

Not that it made any difference; I still loved the area, and was so happy to have moved back. It was a lovely place to bring up our children; but John and I did not like winter, we didn't like the cold wind and the rain. We had spent some lovely holidays in the South of France, and had been there in the spring with lovely balmy weather. We had been told by good authority that the winters were so mild that they didn't drop below sixty degrees.

John would retire at sixty with a full pension, and he said we could afford for me to retire as well, and we would still be young enough to enjoy life. We could sell our house and buy one of the new ones being built in Southern France, which was much cheaper, and we would have a flat in England as a base, because there would be enough money to buy that as well. It was easy to get to France and back, either by car or air, and we could come back when Phil's weekends at home were due, and we would be able to take him back to France for holidays with us too.

There was a business installing CCTV cameras and telephone lines advertised in Florida. It was something that John knew about with all his training at BT, and he was idly reading the article in a newspaper. It flashed through my mind that if we moved to America, I would be nearer to my granddaughter. It might be a few thousand miles away from them, but in America people use planes like taxis.

I urged him to go for the interview. Suddenly a new life in America seemed very exciting; and what a challenge, to run your own business, because I knew I would support him all the way. Phil and Jim could come over for holidays, Andrea would come with us, as would Prince and Charley.

Looking back now I can't believe how easily we were both swept along by this idea. It was most impractical, and we didn't know anything about Florida or whether we would like it there. As for Phil visiting; it would have been much too hot for him.

John went for the interview, and was then flown over to Florida to meet the business owners. He was so buoyant when he returned. He told me about the luxury bungalow set in spacious grounds with its own swimming pool; the business was run from there. He had seen the books, and they had already got established clients, and the profit was good. He had not agreed to buy without asking me; and I trusted him.

I took a few days off, and we flew back so I could see it all. It was exactly as John had described. It was springtime, so the weather was not too hot. Brad and Julia, the couple who were selling it to us, were so charming; they took us out to dinner, and told us how they had such a good relationship with their customers, and how, with a bit of extra input from John, the business would prove to be very lucrative.

We were both totally hooked by now. Andrea liked the idea as well. It was like a drug, a little taste, and then you wanted more; so we signed the papers, and it was all set into motion. We were told it would take about six months to complete, so that gave us ample time to sell the house in England.

We called in an estate agent and put the house up for sale; and from then onwards every single thing went wrong. There was a housing slump and hardly anyone came to view, and we realised we shouldn't have committed ourselves until our house had been sold because we needed that capital. But in spite of this all the paperwork was going through.

That six months went by so quickly; it was now August, and

111

we wanted to do a U-turn. John suddenly realised he was giving up a job that he had worked so hard to get; a BT instructor. I didn't want to leave Crest, but I knew that wherever John went I would want to be with him; this man was my life, and I would be happy anywhere with him. Andrea suddenly announced that she didn't want to go, she wanted to go into sixth form at school. Her GCSE results had been impressive, but all of a sudden it seemed everything was falling apart.

Panic set in, and John even wrote into work to see if his resignation could be retracted, but it was too late. We had cooked our own goose. So he did the only thing he could do, as we had both signed a contract to buy the bungalow and the business, he took out another mortgage. I felt like weeping; we had cleared our mortgage earlier, but as we couldn't sell the house, we had no other choice.

Luckily I had not given my notice in at Crest, and my wages would just cover the mortgage. John would not force Andrea to go; he respected her wish to continue into sixth form, so he sadly told me that he would have to make a start on his own and we would have to follow later. I could fly over for holidays with him every six weeks or so, and he realised that he was going to have to send some money home just to keep us afloat.

Jim had left home by then, and had his own flat, so there was just me and Andrea at home with the animals. I felt devastated that we were being torn apart like this, but I tried to hide it from John; we had to be strong to succeed.

The day I ran him to the airport I struggled to hold back the tears. This man of mine, who had kept me so strong during difficult times, was just about to embark on a new business in a different country. I had encouraged him to do it, and what a fool I was!

By the time I got home, I had stopped feeling sorry for myself; it wasn't going to do me any good, I had to keep this end going whilst he worked at our future. I saw an advertisement in our local free paper for a babysitter with an agency, so I applied for it. I passed the interview, and although I wasn't going to be earning a lot of money, any extra income now would be needed. With all the experience I had been through bringing up my own children, I felt this was a job I could do, and it would fit in with Crest, even if I had to go to some jobs straight from work.

So I kept my head down and worked hard, trying not to remember that we had paid off our mortgage previously and had both had good jobs. It could have been our time to have some nice holidays and be reasonably comfortably off, but we had just blown it!

John used to ring me almost every night when I was home. It was great to hear his voice in the beginning, but one night he told me that we had been conned; Brad and Julia were not the nice couple we had thought, they had deceived us.

Fear rushed through me, whatever did he mean? And then in a broken voice, John explained:

"There is no business left. Once we signed the contracts they stopped taking on work and didn't bother to keep their regulars, they just said they were moving. It looks like they falsified their accounts as well!"

I wish I could say I was surprised by this, but it had been dawning on me for a while that nothing about this was right. We couldn't just give up; John had a mortgage to pay for the bungalow in Florida, or else we would end up homeless in both countries.

"Well you will have to go out and get some new customers, we have to keep going," I said in desperation. I so wished I was there with him to give John the emotional support, and we could have gone out together to get new customers.

"I tried that. I got leaflets printed and I went out to put them through doors, and nearly got arrested; it's illegal to do that out here."

Neither of us had realised that leaflet delivering would be a problem, but we didn't know enough about America; in England everyone does it.

He sounded so depressed, my heart went out to him. He had hoped to send money home to me, and he didn't even have enough to look after himself. I tried to restore his confidence by saying I knew he would find a way, but it just felt that everything was against us.

I took ten of my leave days off from work and the next week flew out to be with him. We were both finding the separation very difficult. Whilst I was there, nothing seemed so bad. A couple of customers from the past had made contact; they wanted work done, which was heartening. John spent time with me; we went out for a meal one evening, and we swam in the pool. We started to make plans for his homecoming at Christmas, which was only a month away.

I flew back home and Jim came to collect me from the airport with Andrea in the car. I told them that dad was doing fine. There was no point in making them worry, and because I am always an optimistic person, I felt sure that these were only teething problems, we would be OK, we had to be!

The next day, when I got up to get ready for work I felt a bit strange. My face felt very stiff. I made myself a cup of tea and sat down to drink it. Andrea was eating her breakfast and reading a book at the same time. This was normal for her. As I lifted the cup up, I went to open my mouth to drink it and I couldn't move my lips. Panic spread through me, whatever was wrong now?

I had to go to work that day because we were short staffed, and I had already been on holiday. I decided to skip breakfast; whatever it was, it would go soon, I was willing it to go. But sometimes that doesn't work, and this was one of those times. Andrea finally noticed something was wrong when I asked her to help me put my lipstick on because I couldn't move my lips. I was scared, but I was trying to fight it, hoping this feeling would wear off.

It was Andrea who persuaded me to go to the doctor. My key holder at work was contacted and she agreed to go in and open up, and I insisted I would be in later. I tried not to speculate about what was wrong with me; the doctor would soon tell me.

My doctor knew straight away. It was Bell's Palsy, a condition that causes the muscles of the face to freeze, usually caused by stress or shock. In my case it had been both, but I didn't say much, the doctor assumed it was because John was away, and I didn't feel like going through our predicament with him.

He explained that it would right itself in a few days, and in the meantime he gave me some facial exercises to do to hasten the recovery. By the time I got into work, I found my mouth had slightly loosened, but the doctor had told me it would be easier to drink through a straw. I think some of the customers must have thought I had just come back from the dentist, and had a frozen mouth, but one of them was a nurse and she asked me what was wrong.

I told her it was Bell's Palsy, and her response wasn't exactly heartening.

"Oh, my sister-in-law had that, and her face stayed all twisted, her mouth was always lopsided."

I looked at her in horror; what a Job's comforter. Maybe I shouldn't have told her.

"Well, I am going to do exercises, and my face won't stay like that!" I said firmly.

The next day there was a meeting for managers over at our head office at Crayford. It couldn't have been at a worse time as far as I was concerned; but I wasn't an invalid, I was determined to go. My speech was a little slurred, so I hoped no one thought I was drunk, and I used a straw for drinks like I had been told. Nobody made any comment, but I think that was thanks to Liam. I had told him in private why I had been to the doctor, and he may well have asked everyone to be discreet.

I did not tell John about this, because he didn't need any extra worry, and after about a week my face was back to normal. It was such a relief. The doctor had said it usually only happens to someone once, so hopefully it would never come back again.

Chapter Sixteen

John remained in Florida for eight months, doing his best to keep the business afloat. But he had no money to pay Brad for the mortgage on the bungalow. He had to weather the telephone calls from Brad, who shouted down the line: "Get out of my house!"

So he left the house and the business and came home. He was a broken man, convinced that he had failed us all. To me the money didn't matter. I didn't care any more about what we had lost; he was back home. As long as we were together, then I could cope. Maybe we would be poor for the rest of our lives, but we had each other, and I still had my job.

I told him that I was as much to blame for encouraging him to go for the business in the first place, but now we had to move on, and he must stop feeling guilty. What was done was done, and we still had the rest of our lives in front of us, and importantly we still had our home, even though it was now remortgaged.

We flew back to America just once more to meet with an American attorney. We told him the whole story, and he agreed with us that Brad and Julia had definitely acted unprofessionally and taken advantage of us, particularly as we had purchased the business in good faith. It had been their duty to keep it going for those six months, and not to close it down. He also told us that proving it could be very difficult and would cost a lot of money, and there was no guarantee we would win the case.

So we had no choice but to accept what we couldn't change, and move on. All we could hope for was karma, that one day someone would do to them what they had done to us; not that we would ever know about it.

After a week or so John's mojo returned, he got some leaflets printed by a local shop advertising himself for painting the outside of people's houses, and he delivered them all around the area. Within a few days the telephone rang, and he was getting bookings. Nowadays someone wanting any sort of work would probably post on FaceBook or Twitter, such is the power of social media, but in the early nineties we didn't have a home computer, I am not sure many people did.

So we managed to keep afloat. I was so grateful that I was doing a job I loved, and I knew that John must have found it hard to go from being a BT Instructor with a good wage, to painting and decorating, but he never said anything. More work came in for him, decorating the inside of houses too, and odd jobs. At weekends he did mini-cabbing. He worked at night whilst I was out babysitting, but I always turned down work on Sundays, that was our one day together and it was very precious to me.

Now that there was only Andrea at home, we had three spare bedrooms, so we took in three lodgers. I cooked an evening meal for everyone, and luckily the three men were out all day. Two of them were teachers, the other one was a student at college. I hated sharing our home with other people, but now we needed the extra income.

By the time she was seventeen, Andrea had decided that she didn't want to carry on with her sixth form course. She now wanted to be independent, just like her sister before her, and leave home.

I think it's hardest when your youngest child goes, because they will always be your baby. John was devastated, he had always tried to keep her safe, and because she was the child he always thought he couldn't have, she had been extra precious to him. But sometimes it's hard to say the words you want to say, like "Please don't go." He knew he would miss her; we both would.

He was always worried some sort of harm would come to her. I was also very upset, but we had to respect the fact that it was her choice. She wanted to stand on her own two feet, which was to be applauded, but it left a huge void in our lives. My dad was concerned too, but I tried to make light of it, saying she was fine, it was all good experience for her, and tried to believe that myself. She was going to be sharing a flat with four other girls, friends of a similar age, so maybe it would be good for her, who could tell? I know that I definitely would not have been mature enough at seventeen to leave home. I never did have a flat, I lived with my parents until I got married at nineteen.

Silk Screen Arts closed down, and Jim was made redundant. He kept himself busy selling Kleeneze products for a while, and then found himself a job as a night watchman. The pay was poor, and he had to work about seventy-two hours a week just to earn enough to pay his rent and eat, but he was so anxious to be gainfully employed he put up with it.

Our lodgers moved away to teach at other schools. This meant we just had the student left, so we started hosting foreign students again. Because we had none of our children living in the house, it was the teachers that were sent to us.

Phil reached his twenty-first birthday; an age which doctors had never expected him to reach, but he had always been a fighter. He was much healthier now thanks to modern medication. He was happy, and all the meltdowns, and self harming stopped. He had become a very happy young man, enjoying life at his own pace.

It's natural for every parent to want the very best for their child in life. I knew that Phil could never lead a normal life; go to work, get married and have children, but I still had him, and he really loved his life, so I felt grateful for that. Happiness is the most important thing in life. Phil was happy, and he took everything in his stride. I thought about all the years he had been in and out of hospital so many times, and all the illnesses he had conquered, and I felt incredibly proud of him.

I thought back to the time he had been born, and I had realised he was different from my other children and would need special help. I would love to have had something to read to help guide me along the way. It was all trial and error for us as a family. Thinking these thoughts encouraged me to do something about it, and I sat down and wrote all our experiences out by hand. My intention was to send it to Mencap, so they could put it in their magazine.

When Mencap read it they said it should be a book, as there were not enough books around about this subject. They gave me the contact details of my publisher, United Writers of Cornwall, so I wrote off to them, explaining what I had written.

The reply came back that they would be interested in reading it, but it must be submitted in typewritten form. I couldn't type, but I was going to have to learn. So John and I went to a secondhand shop and bought a typewriter. I realised I was going to have to type it out, even if it was with two fingers.

My day started at seven o'clock, when we awoke and got ready for work, but I started waking up at five, and spent two hours typing each morning, and then another couple of hours in the evening. It took me six weeks to type it out, and when I submitted it I was hoping they had waited for me as they only had a few vacant slots a year for new work.

A reply came back through the post fairly quickly. The editor had accepted my work, but made the point that it should really have been double spaced. If only he'd known the work that had gone into my typing it! I have made sure ever since, that all my work is double spaced.

I was so excited about having a book published. I had always kept it quiet from our directors at work that I had a child with so many difficulties, as I thought they would think I might be unreliable, but now it was all out in the open. They were very kind to me, and I had lots of orders from directors and shop staff within the company. I also had a market within secondary schools for their libraries, as the aim was to bring children with autism into schools together with more able pupils, with extra help when it was needed. Not only did it make the secondary school pupils aware that some other children have special needs, and need patience and understanding, it also encouraged the children with autism to be like their peers.

In November 1992 Anita gave birth to her second daughter, Katelyn, who has always been known as Katey. No longer could John and I afford for both of us to go to visit them in America, so he stayed at home and looked after the animals whilst I went. He understood how important it was for me to keep that contact with Anita and the little ones, as they grow up so very quickly.

Anita was a natural mother. She combined motherhood with keeping her home immaculately clean, and she was also still running and competing. As well as this she was studying at home for her degree in Physical Education, which she hoped to put to good use when the children were older and she would be able to return to work.

During that first year of Katey's life, Tom's job took him away from home more than he wanted. He was flying helicopters and doing endurance tests. He was sorry to miss her early months of development, but Anita kept everything running smoothly at home.

In 1994 Anita became pregnant again, and in April 1995 Ashley was born. She was ten weeks early, and on the first night, Tom sat by her cot all night willing her to live. She only weighed about three pounds. Luckily she did pull through, and I have noticed over the years that she has inherited her mother's fun loving and zany sense of humour.

So now they had three beautiful daughters, but Tom jokingly complained that he was surrounded by women and would love to have a son. Anita said they would have one more try for a boy, as after all her mum had managed with four children, and was still here to tell the tale!

In 1996, during my visit to Anita and Tom, she did a triathlon, which involved running, swimming and cycling. She was competing alongside men as well, and she beat most of them. In her female category, she was a runaway winner. I marvelled at the way she managed to have babies, look after them so well, and keep herself so fit. Maybe the answer was that ever since being a little girl, she had always been so well disciplined.

During that year she became pregnant again. The baby was due in June 1997, and the plan was for me to wait until it was born, and then book my yearly flight to come over and help her in the early weeks. But before the year of 1996 was over, my life was to change drastically in many ways.

Chapter Seventeen

When I became a manager back in 1985, I hired new staff and they stayed with me. I took on Saturday boys; they were sixth form pupils so they changed every couple of years. The customers loved to be served by these lads, and often they carried their goods to the car. Over the years our shop flourished, we hit all our targets, and although Crest had about ten branches in all, ours was definitely up there as one of the best. I was proud of my staff; they always looked smart, and treated the customers with a courtesy that you don't always find in shops today.

But from about 1995 our takings plummeted, and of course it worried me, so we tried even harder to please our customers to keep their loyalty. It was also happening to the other branches; the tastes of the public were changing. No longer were their tables adorned with the finest Waterford crystal, or beautiful Wedgwood and Royal Doulton china. Plain glass became the fashion, also plain white everyday, earthenware china.

We stocked David Winter and Lilliput Lane cottages, but they also went out of fashion. We also had Swarovski crystal, and so many beautiful but luxury goods. None of them were essential, so when people were trying to cut back and economise, it was the luxury goods market that suffered.

One of our bosses from head office, named John, came over to deliver the sad news that within a few weeks we would be made redundant. That shop had been a big part of my life for sixteen years. Going to work had kept me sane at times when I was under huge pressure, and the money I earned had been a godsend. On

f

the day I locked the door and set the alarm for the last time, I felt such a sadness deep inside, it was the end of an era, and it had been a very happy one.

During that time I wrote another story. There was an advert in the Sunday paper for authors manuscripts wanted, so I replied, my manuscript was accepted, and it was published on 4th June 1996 in paperback. But in the meantime the company closed down and my book became out of print and no longer available. I learned the hard way that not all publishers can be trusted. So anyone out there with a story they want published, it's probably best to publish it through Amazon; I have heard you can do this for nothing.

But then something good happened. John had seen a job advertisement for a caretaker at a local school. It held a certain amount of responsibility, as the school was for boys with emotional and behavioural problems; lots of them were disruptive, and it would be quite a challenge.

He went for the interview and got the job. His first words to me were, "It's a good wage, we can stop hosting the students and their teachers, have our own space at home back again, and you can go back to working part time if you want to."

I gave him a hug. I was so proud that he had got this job out of over sixty applicants, and it had boosted his confidence too. He could now leave behind mini-cabbing and decorating, and do a job he would probably really enjoy.

After spending all those years in retail I wasn't sure what I could do at the age of fifty-two. I liked the thought of having Saturdays off again, but selling was one thing I seemed to be quite good at. One evening I went babysitting for a family of three children that I knew well. I told their mother, Sue, that I had just been made redundant, and intended to hunt for a part time job soon.

"I know just the job for you, Carol, my friend has three children, and she wants to return to work. She is a counsellor for people affected by cancer. It's a very important job, but she is nervous about leaving her children with someone she knows nothing about. I can tell her about you."

I looked at her in amazement. Would someone want a fifty-two year old as a nanny? Was it really going to be that easy? Up until now, nothing in the past had been that easy.

Chris Jacobs invited me to go round to her house at Chislehurst for an interview. She had three delightful children; Robbie was six, Emma four, and Michael was nearly two. I liked the idea of looking after them. The eldest two were at school, so I would take and collect them each day. I would look after Michael all day, and he turned out to be such a contented little boy who loved playing with his cars. The job was three days a week; Tuesday, Wednesday and Thursday.

Sue had obviously spoken very kindly about me, as Chris offered me the job that same day, and after I had discussed it with John, I accepted it. Then Chris said they were thinking of having a puppy, would I have any objection? I have always loved dogs, I was brought up with them, and I said I didn't mind at all, and would walk the dog with Michael after I had taken the children to school.

They bought a collie puppy, and they named him Jake. I loved that dog as if he was my own, and often looked after him if they went away so he didn't need to be put in kennels. Our Prince was now twelve years old and still fairly fit for his age, and a couple of times I took him with me to work, as neither John nor I wanted to leave him all day at home.

Life seemed to be really looking up for us now. John was enjoying his job. The headmaster told him that the last caretaker had built a barbecue for the boys to enjoy, but some of them had vandalised and spoilt it. Being always up for a challenge, John said that he would build another one, and this time the boys could take turns in helping him, then maybe if they had put some effort into it, they wouldn't be so destructive.

A few of the boys had already sought him out and chatted to him, so he was trying to build some sort of relationship with them, but he knew it wouldn't be easy, as they were boys who had suffered emotionally or been neglected in their lives up to then. They didn't know who to trust, but John was very keen to try and win them over.

I was enjoying my job too, and with all the children now gone, it was our time. We had a bit more money, we could take some nice holidays and maybe go out to the theatre sometimes. There was always a feeling of loss that Andrea had left home, but as long as she was happy in her new life, we had to respect that.

But life is strange, you can be right on top of a mountain one minute, and then down in the depths of the deepest hole. Life is one big roller coaster, we just go round and round, and we can't seem to get off.

We were feeling particularly happy. I was soon to have my fourth grandchild, and Chris was happy enough about me going to America in June. As a mother she understood how important that visit would be, both for me and for Anita.

In late February 1997, Anita rang me and she explained that Tom had now left the navy, as he didn't like travelling away from home and missing all the milestones that the girls hit. He had passed his interview to join the FBI, and they were holding a celebration party the next week. Now that he wouldn't be posted to so many different places, they were going to buy their own house. The mortgage had been approved, and they planned to live in Richmond, Virginia. She was bubbling over with excitement, and said how pleased she was that I would be there with her when her new baby had been born. Scans were only just becoming available, but she had just had one and knew she was carrying another little girl. She said they were going to call the baby Emily, which is one of my favourite names; it was also my mother's middle name.

The next week it had been my turn to ring her, which I did, but there was no reply. Then I remembered she had said they would be at the celebration at FBI headquarters. Tom's mum Carol had also gone, and I wished I had been able to as well, but it was more important for me to be there when the baby was born.

Although John had been at his job for a few weeks now, he had been told there would be a police check, just because he was working with young vulnerable boys. We had no worries about that, it was normal procedure, so when there was a knock at the door and he opened it to see two men in uniform, he jokingly said: "Don't mind Prince, he'll only lick you to death."

"Is your wife about?" came the immediate reply.

When the policemen came in, I could see by their faces they had something serious to say. I knew in that instance, when the cold hand of fear clutched at my heart, that something was terribly wrong. One of them looked at me, his face very grave.

"You need to sit down Mrs Creasey. I am afraid we have some very sad news for you."

My heart was thudding so loudly, I felt it would burst through my chest. John had instinctively moved over and put his arm around my shoulders. I saw the policeman's lips move, and I heard his words, but my confused brain could not take in and digest what he was saying.

"I am afraid there has been a car crash in Richmond, and sadly your daughter has lost her life."

"N-ooooo!" I heard John say, as he collapsed on my shoulder sobbing with grief. He had always worried that Andrea would come to some harm when she left home. She was a beautiful young girl, who was very naïve, and he frequently said she could be raped or murdered if she went out at night on her own; she could be laying dead in a ditch and we wouldn't know. So in his troubled mind, he assumed she had been in that car at Richmond, and so did I.

But then the policeman continued.

"Luckily her two little girls survived, the eldest one was in another car with her dad."

And then it struck me; it wasn't Andrea, it was Anita! But my mind fought back. It couldn't be Anita; she was over six months pregnant, she was a careful driver, she always knew what she was doing in life, and she had a great future ahead of her. Somebody like her, so full of life and energy, a girl who was so sunny, inside and out, and everyone loved her. How could cruel fate extinguish her life in an instant and yet there were murderers in prison who would go on living?

I don't remember much more about the conversation. There seemed to be a blank wall around me. I opened my mouth to speak, but I couldn't, I had lost my voice. I could feel John holding me tightly, saying what a tragedy it was. Anita and the baby; he couldn't believe it, and I couldn't believe it either. My little girl, she was only twenty-nine, she had barely started living her life, and her baby Emily, who would never get a chance to even start her life; they had gone, just like that.

Chapter Eighteen

1997 was definitely the worst year of my life. We had spent years living on a knife-edge, never sure whether Phil would reach adulthood, but we never dreamed that Anita, who was healthy and strong with her whole life ahead of her, would die at twenty-nine.

Anyone reading this would understand the grief that assaults you. I wished I had told her how proud of her I was, and how much I loved her during our last conversation. I also wished I had given more of my time to her, but she was always so independent, and totally focused on what she wanted. So many things I wished, but it was too late, she was gone.

How do you tell your other children they have lost their sibling? Well I couldn't. The huge shock had rendered me speechless. Some mothers weep and wail when they lose a child, a strange unearthly sound that comes from deep within; it's like part of yourself has died; but I was struck dumb, and I wept silent tears of anguish.

John managed to get hold of Jim and Andrea, and she came over with her partner at that time, Andrew, immediately. She adored her sister, as did Jim, and we banded together, as families do, scarcely able to believe that such a bright light that Anita was had been brutally extinguished.

My behaviour at this time was irrational. Being unable to speak, I craved to have some sort of connection with her, so out came the photograph albums of when she was born, right up to the present time. I spent all weekend looking at them; but when that weekend was over, I put them away, and couldn't bear to see her. It was four years before I could speak her name without crying, my beautiful girl was gone forever.

Although upset, John was more together than I was. He found out that the FBI in America had contacted the police in England, because Tom was too heartbroken to be able to tell us. Everyone in America was in a state of shock. She had been driving behind his mother's car, as Tom had taken someone else to the airport. Becky was in the car with Tom, which probably saved her life. Nobody was going fast, and Anita had her babies with her, Ashley in the front and Katey in the back, both in their baby seats. It was a hot afternoon, and Anita was tired, she had one of the windows down slightly. The car simply left the road and ended upside down in a field. No other car was involved. They said she must have died instantly, and baby Emily too, and I am grateful that she didn't suffer. So beware of falling asleep at the wheel, because we think that is what happened, just briefly nodding off, and then losing control of the steering wheel.

Ashley, although in the front, didn't have a mark on her, whereas four year old Katey in the back broke her leg, and it was so bad they had to pin it, and she had to learn to walk again. But the emotional damage of losing her mother was far greater than any physical pain, and for months afterwards she had nightmares.

Mick was as heartbroken as me. He had remarried by now, and I was so relieved that he had Joan to support him. The FBI flew me out, and the others went on another plane together. John was upset, as knowing how scared of flying I am, he felt we should have been together. I could feel nothing; I was numb and disconnected from it all. I suppose in times of unbearable grief, it is nature's way of getting you through it.

The FBI were very involved with the funeral. A procession of cars drove to the church, and many of the people that Anita and Tom had met over the years when he was posted to different areas came to pay their respects.

The one thing I had done before we left England was to write to our local paper and inform them of her death. The reason they knew of her was because she had been presented to the Mayor for all her sporting achievements, and for when her relay team broke the British record. These events had been on local news and in the newspapers. They did a write-up about her, and apparently got a huge response from people who knew her.

127

I don't remember much about the funeral. I know John was there beside me, always my rock, and Jim and Andrea were in the aisle behind. As the coffin slowly progressed down the aisle, I found it hard to comprehend that my beautiful girl was inside it, and I remember my dear Jim, who is not normally one to show much emotion, clasping my hand from behind, and saying:

"Mum, I know how you feel. Mum, we'll get through this."

I wasn't just grieving for myself, but for the whole family; her siblings, her father, her husband, and her small children who had to grow up without a mother. Tom was devastated, but the brave front he put on for his children was to be commended. I was still in a daze, but I was being selfish in my grief. I knew it wasn't all about me, and he needed my help; so I volunteered to stay on for another three weeks to try and help the children find some sort of normality.

Chris understood, and arranged for a temporary nanny to cover my absence. John had to go back to work, as did Jim and Andrea; she was working in the office of an aircraft company now. That three weeks was tough. Katey woke up screaming from terrifying nightmares almost every night. Becky was just seven, and she felt her mother's loss tremendously, saying no one could cook anything she wanted like her mum had.

Ashley was still in nappies and not talking much yet, but she cried for "Momma" continually, so I took her out for walks to try and distract her. The neighbours were very kind; the last thing you think about when you are grieving is eating, and they visited with meals that just needed heating up.

This was definitely a family in crisis. The girls were so young, they didn't deserve to lose their mum so tragically, and Tom was going to have to try and balance his job at the FBI whilst bringing up his daughters. He spoke about having a daily nanny to look after Ashley and get the others off to school. He didn't want a live-in one, he wanted to keep their privacy. I knew Carol would help as much as she could, and they were staying at her house at that time, but Tom was planning to buy his own accommodation nearby. Carol was not in the best of health and couldn't afford to have too much stress, but any ideas about Tom and the children living in Richmond had now been dismissed; they needed to stay in Greensboro.

By the end of the three weeks I was missing John so much; I

needed his strength to lean on. Nevertheless, I also felt very bad about leaving my grandchildren. It seemed to me that I was the nanny that came and went, not the one who was constant in their lives, and I would go back to England and leave them again. Before I went I told them that I hoped to be back to see them soon.

When I saw John waiting for me at the airport I noticed how tired he looked. His face relaxed when he saw me, and I felt the comfort of his strong arms around me. On the way home he spoke about the huge response there had been from past friends of Anita at the news of her death. He suggested something I had not even thought of, a memorial service to celebrate Anita's short but very inspirational life. She may have lived for only twenty-nine years, but she had packed so much into that time and achieved so much, then so sadly died before she could complete her degree.

So we set about arranging a special celebration of her life, and it was announced in the local newspaper. Mick came with his mother Joan, and also his brother Roger with his wife Yvonne. Tony and his wife Bette, my dad, Ron, Audrey and Betty were also there. When we stood inside the church greeting people, I could not believe the number of Anita's young friends who came along. She had been successful as both a swimmer and a runner, so most of Beckenham Swimming Club was there, and Bromley Ladies running club. Then there were her friends from school, including Linda, her very best friend from early days. I always think it's sad when someone dies they don't know how loved they were; or do they?

Chris suggested I take three months off work, but I knew that wouldn't do for me. I had to keep busy and occupy my mind with other things. Her children seemed to love me and their cuddles and hugs were comforting. I worked for three days, but on my other days I shut myself away, not wanting to see anyone, being strong on the outside was something I could only keep up whilst at work.

John must have said something to his headmaster, because he told me that the school had said if I wanted to drive over at any time and have a cup of tea with him, they didn't mind. So I did this, and he showed me the barbecue he was building with help from the boys. It was half completed and nobody had tried to vandalise it so far. He was enthusiastic about the project because he himself had come from a one parent family and had a difficult upbringing with no father around. He understood that some children become maladjusted because of circumstances, and he had an empathy for them. His mother had been married to a man who led a double life with another family, and his father had committed bigamy when he married her, then left them.

Back in 1975, just before I gave birth to Andrea, John had met his father, whom he had not seen since he was seven years old, and he said it had meant nothing; he could feel no ties to him. His mother had been told, and expressed a wish to see him, but both John and his brother Malcolm had been worried that all their father wanted was to upset their mum's life, so they had not divulged her address.

When Andrea was born, John's mum, Betty, was delighted when we took her to visit, but she died when Andrea was five years old. Years later, when I asked Andrea if she could remember her, she said she could not recall what she looked like, but she did remember being given a beaded purse by her, which she had kept in a special place.

One of the finest things about John was that he cared about people who were less fortunate than himself; that was probably why he was able to support me emotionally. He wasn't a perfect person, but then neither am I. He was bossy and obstinate, but so am I; and his finest quality was that behind his strong tough exterior, after growing up as a latch key kid, he cared.

Our Prince was now thirteen, and we could see him slowing down. He needed help with his back legs now; it is so sad when you see a family pet declining. I let him out in the garden one morning and I noticed he was stumbling, so I took him to the vet. I was told he probably had a brain tumour, and was now blind, and he was too old to cope with an operation. The vet said we would have to let him go, so I brought him home. When John returned from work, I told him all about it, knowing that losing Prince, his faithful friend, was going to devastate him. We all loved dear Prince, but he was John's shadow, he followed him everywhere.

John took him to the vet when I was at work, and he was put peacefully to sleep. My poor husband was beside himself with grief, and he brought Prince back in a wheelbarrow and buried him deep in the garden along with his ball. It was yet another heartbreak to cope with.

Chapter Nineteen

John's grief over losing Prince was profound. He had been more than a dog, he was a greatly loved family member, and his loyalty towards all of us was touching. To John he had been his shadow. Animals often attach themselves to a certain person, and I think Prince was so grateful to be rescued from all the abuse he had suffered, that those two hours in the garden with John on his first day made him realise most humans are kind, and this cemented their bond.

I didn't really feel we needed another dog. I looked after Jake quite a bit if Chris and Ian went away, and then I spent three days a week looking after him as part of my job. John had declared that there could never be another dog like Prince, so I was surprised when he expressed a wish to go to 'Last Chance' at Edenbridge and save a dog.

I decided that if it was going to help with his grief, then I really didn't mind, so we went to view the dogs. The first thing that impressed me when we opened the gate to enter the rescue centre, was a courtyard with many dogs walking about freely, all very friendly and welcoming. When the lady booked us in she explained that these were the dogs who lived there all the time because they had never been homed. None of them had issues, and some had been rejected simply because they were not 'pretty enough'.

She explained that as they now lived at the home, it wasn't fair to keep them in wire pens, so they had their freedom to roam about the courtyard, and there was always a chance that someone entering would want to take one of them home. I was impressed to hear this, and wished I could take them all home!

In the first pen was a collie, and also a large but very beautiful dog. It was brindle; the gold shimmering in the sun beneath its dark brown fur. It was an Alsatian retriever cross, and it seemed full of fun, and was busy romping with the collie in the pen. It was quite a big dog, I thought maybe a bit too big for us.

We looked around at all the other dogs but none were really suitable. We had to consider Charley; it had to be a dog that was friendly towards cats and wouldn't chase her. But I knew instinctively which dog would have appealed to John, and his next words confirmed this.

"I don't know what you think, but there are no puppies here that would respect Charley from the onset. The brindle dog in the first pen is very striking."

"I knew you would choose that one. It is a beautiful dog," I admitted.

So they took it out of the pen, and we were told she was a girl and her name was Shimmer. We took her for a walk and fell in love with her. She was very affectionate, and we asked how they thought she would react to a cat; as she was not a puppy, she was two and a half years old.

This rescue centre had cats as well, so Shimmer was taken into the part where they were and told not to chase, and she didn't, and the lady explained that we might well find our cat would rule her, because when the cats hissed, she ran well away from them.

So we took a chance, and chose her. And what a good choice she was. We were not allowed to take her on the first day, as they had to check us out to make sure we were suitable. John was going to collect her on the next day, and I suddenly thought how lonely the collie would be after Shimmer went, so I asked him what he thought about having the collie as well. However, when he returned with her, he told me that someone else had claimed the collie, which was probably for the best as we could only really afford to have one dog.

She sat on the back seat of the car, without fidgeting, all the way home. They had explained that she had been neglected. She had been slung out of the house all day whilst the man went to work, and not fed properly. When the police took her back after finding her roaming the streets, the man swore and said he didn't want her, so she had ended up at the rescue centre. It was plain to see that someone had loved her once, because she was trained to walk at heel and wait at roads, but whoever they were, and for whatever reason, they were no longer a part of her life.

We renamed her Purdie, and right from the start it was me she followed around. John commented that she was going to be my dog rather than his, but he didn't mind. We both felt that the house seemed complete now we had a dog in it, and right from the very start, Purdie and Charley got on really well.

Chris suggested that I bring her to work with me. Jake was a very lively collie, and together the two dogs had the time of their lives. When they had run themselves ragged, they used to fall asleep and Jake would rest his head next to Purdie; he absolutely adored her, but it was definitely Purdie who wore the trousers in their relationship. She was a big dog, and during their play fights she used to pin him down, with mock growling going on. In the beginning I was worried she might hurt him, but he loved every minute of it.

With such a busy job, three lively children, and two dogs to take care of, it didn't leave me much time to indulge my grief. Keeping busy really helped, and I spent the weekend at home with John, and on Mondays and Fridays I drove over to the school to see him for a while; it was something to look forward to, and broke the day up a bit for me.

Jim and Andrea were grieving too, so I tried to keep myself together for them. Nevertheless, I have found over the years, that no matter how occupied I am during the day, I still think of Anita every day, and I think that is important no matter how much it hurts. When we lose someone, we should keep their memory alive. They should never be forgotten.

So the days passed, and it was now early June, just under three months since we had lost her. I was in contact with Tom and I knew it wasn't easy for him. Finding a daytime nanny that was reliable, and also prepared to accept that the girls needed a lot of understanding, was hard, and he had to balance his job with all that.

Before Anita's death, John had been talking about doing up the kitchen. It needed repainting and generally brightening up, but when the tragedy happened, everything else was forgotten. In an effort to try and resume normality, he mentioned it again to me. It was on a Monday night as were going to bed.

"Yes, I suppose so," I said, but without the enthusiasm I normally had when we were redecorating.

"I'll try not to be too messy," grinned John, and I mentally shook myself; he was doing it for me, how ungrateful was I?

"It's a good idea, what colour do you think it should be?" I asked him; and then I saw his face change, he screwed it up slightly, and still being vulnerable, I was scared.

"John, what's wrong, are you OK?"

"I don't feel quite right. Maybe I am tired, I am going to bed."

Once in bed, I cuddled up close to him. I had only survived the loss of Anita because of his support and strength. This man was my rock, and with his help I would get through it, because I couldn't change what fate had thrown at us. I was relieved to hear his even breathing. He must have been tired, as he had fallen asleep immediately.

The next day was Tuesday, and John declared himself as fit as a fiddle, and went off to work. I followed an hour later, with Purdie. Tuesday was my first day of the week with Chris. When I returned home that evening John was in, and he had started dinner. He was making what we called a microwave casserole; left over meat from Sunday cooked with mixed vegetables and thick gravy, accompanied by mashed potato. Since everyone had left home, he had turned his hand to do a bit of cooking, and it was nice when I arrived home to find that dinner was almost ready.

During the evening I reminded him that the next day I would be in late, as I was babysitting straight after work. The lady I was sitting for would leave a salad meal for me, as she knew I was going straight from work, and I expected to be home about ten o'clock.

John was used to the funny hours that I kept, and I had left him a meal he could heat up. I was going to bring Purdie back when I went to collect the children from school, and he would take her for a walk when he came in at five o'clock.

So the next day, which was Wednesday 4th June, we both went off to work. John always brought me up a cup of tea as he was leaving. I was very sleepy that morning, but he kissed me goodbye, and said he was going to look at paint colours for the kitchen after work, and he would share the leaflets with me later when I came in, and then we could decide.

Marina Bray was the lady I was babysitting for. Marina and her husband Peter worked in the city, and they liked to go out to dinner straight after work sometimes, and then come home about nine thirty. They had a son and a daughter and I had been working for them for several years, and the children knew me well.

I got the children off to bed, read them their bedtime stories, then sat down. It had been a long and busy day, so when Peter and Marina came in we had a brief chat, and then I got in the car to go home. When I arrived home, I could see the house was all in darkness, and that was a surprise. John hadn't said anything about going out. When I opened the door, Purdie rushed out of the gloom, tail wagging, and then ran into the garden for a wee.

I could feel a huge panic sweeping over me, even though I was fighting to control it. A glance inside the microwave confirmed he had not been home; the meal was still in there. I came back into the hall, only to see Derek from across the road, who was a close friend of John, and happened to be a policeman, walking towards our front door.

I was silent, but I could hear a voice inside me screaming, no, no, I can't take any more stress! I opened the door to Derek and he came in. He was a kindly man with a round jolly face, always smiling, but the look on his face then was anguish, and I could recognise immediately how uncomfortable he felt. Whatever he had to say to me wasn't going to be nice, I just knew it.

"I have been out babysitting, I thought John would be in," I explained.

Derek's voice shook, and I have never seen him more serious than that moment when he spoke to me.

"Carol, I don't know how to tell you this after you have so recently lost Anita. . ."

Instinctively I covered my ears; of course it was a coward's way out, but I had lost all my courage.

"Don't give me any more bad news Derek, I can't take it!" I implored him, but he carried on, he had to, it was his job.

"I am afraid that John was found on the ground at work today. An ambulance was called, but he was pronounced dead on arrival at Bromley Hospital."

"He can't be dead. He's fit and well, and only fifty-three!" I burst out, not being able to comprehend what he was saying.

"They are doing a post mortem, and will give you the results, of course."

Then he clasped my hand: "I knew hours ago. It happened about two o'clock, but we didn't know where you were. I just kept coming over here, and I couldn't get Purdie out because the door was locked."

I heard his words, but my mind was desperately trying to make some sense of them. This couldn't be happening to me again, I had just buried my daughter; how cruel fate was! What had I done in my life that was so bad that I had to lose my husband as well? I loved him so much, he was my world, and I had expected we would grow old together.

By now Derek had taken control; the kettle was on, and he made me sit down. Then he asked if I wanted him to contact Jim and Andrea. Here I was again in crisis, and they had to be told the worst news ever.

I don't remember too much about what happened next, except that even though the evening was late, they were very soon with me. Derek didn't go home until he knew that I wouldn't be on my own. My world felt like it was collapsing around me, but it's in times like this that family bonds matter, and we all leaned on each other in an effort to cope with it. Suddenly I felt as if nothing would ever be the same again, my darling was gone forever.

Chapter Twenty

I was so lucky that, at probably the most traumatic time in my life, Andrew took up the reins to help me with everything. He did all my paperwork and arranged the funeral, but doing it in a way that I was able to make all the decisions. Derek and his wife Pat, as well as our next door neighbours Martin and Michele, told me not to worry about the catering side of things. I dutifully left everything to them, as we had a lot of people coming. They begged, borrowed, and somehow got together a lot of tables and chairs, which were ranged around the garden, as luckily it was a fine day. I can't remember what the meal was, because I was finding it hard to eat at the time and ended up losing two stone in weight, but they did me proud. Derek asked if he could do an address about John at the service, as he felt he knew him well, and I welcomed his input.

John's ex-wife and their daughters had been contacted, and invited to the funeral. I felt the very last thing I could do for John was to welcome them to the service, and to our home, and as a gesture of goodwill, I invited them to travel in the funeral car with me and my family.

A few days after John's death, the headmaster from the school he worked at came to see me, to offer his condolences. He spoke very warmly about my husband, which eased my grief slightly, as I wanted everyone to remember him with kindness. He said how the boys at the school had liked him, and shown a willingness to help him build the barbecue. He had got through to them, and impressed everyone with his way of dealing with them. He also told me that although John had only been at his job for three months, as his widow, they were going to pay me a year's worth of his wages. I thanked him, but at that moment money meant very little to me.

Chris had also been round with carrier bags of food she had bought for us. When you are grieving, you lose your appetite, yet you need all your strength to deal with your loss even though eating is the last thing on your mind. There were also prepared meals to encourage me to eat, and I did try, even though I felt continually nauseous.

John had always disliked the colour black; he liked bright colours, and so I asked everyone to celebrate his life by not wearing black. John's daughters had asked if they could say a few words about him; they were missing him so much, so I was happy to let them. I was determined that this day was going to be all about supporting one another in our grief, and it was going to go smoothly.

I will never forget my dad. He was by now eighty-eight years old, but he drove up from Herne Bay and stood holding my hand as we walked into the church behind the coffin. Ron, Jimmy and Andrea were also with us, and John's other daughters were behind with their mother. My dad had long since admitted he had been wrong about John, and by then had huge respect for him.

The pews were lined with people John had worked with, friends of us both, his relatives, including his brother Malcolm, who was himself older than John, together with his new bride Editha. There were also representatives of Beckenham Swimming Club, as John had been a swimming instructor there for many years.

Derek spoke very glowingly about John, saying that he had cared about people who were less fortunate than himself. He told some humorous tales about how himself, John and other neighbours had stood out in the front garden trying to put the world to rights, and he also spoke about how devastated John had been when Anita died, closely followed by his faithful Prince, who had been his shadow. He said that, for sure, Prince would have been reunited with his master now in a better place.

Then John's daughters stood up and spoke about how much they loved their dad, what a good man he had been, and how unfair that he should die at fifty-three. It was very moving, as they wept as they said the words. My heart went out to them, they had said what we were all thinking; it just wasn't fair!

John was cremated; that had been his wish, and the vicar had agreed that his ashes could be buried in the churchyard. I must confess that I wasn't a churchgoer. I have always believed in God, and I have thanked God for what I have, and prayed to him when I need comfort and support, but always at home. My definition of a Christian is someone who treats others with kindness.

I desperately tried to carry on as normal, knowing in my heart that nothing would ever be normal again. When Anita and baby Emily died I felt as if part of me had been ripped out; and now John. I couldn't say which loss was the worse; my daughter who grew inside me, or my husband who was my soulmate. My heart was full of pain, and I didn't see how I could ever lead any sort of happy life again, because emotionally I was a mess, truly heartbroken.

This was how I felt inside. But I think when things like this happen, God gives us an inner strength so we can face the world. Because whether we like it or not, life does go on, even though I then felt that it shouldn't.

So I carried on doing my babysitting. It wasn't that I needed the money now, but most of the people I sat for had become friends, and knew exactly what had happened. During one of our conversations Marina said to me:

"After what has happened to you in the last few months, Carol, it must be hard for you to believe in God."

"I still believe," I assured her, and I did. As grief-stricken as I was, I did get through everything, and it wasn't just me or all my supportive friends and family that got me through, it was a force stronger than that. God was with me at that terrible time in every way.

A few days after the funeral, the following Saturday, Andrea and Andrew were there. They had taken to staying the weekends with me so I wouldn't be alone, but when they realised that I was going out babysitting as usual, and I assured them I would be OK, they went home. Their thoughtfulness at such a time was so very kind. I am not sure if I thanked Andrea at the time, but I am thanking her now. I love you. xx

It is amazing how kind people can be when you feel low. Not long after the funeral, Pablo, a Spanish student that we had hosted in 1996 wrote to me. Well, the letter was addressed to both of us, saying how much he had enjoyed his stay last year, and how were we both?

It would have been very easy just to reply and say fine, as I didn't expect to see him again, but I wrote back and told him about John. We had by then received the results of the post mortem. John had suffered a blood clot, an unnaturally large one, and it had stopped his heart instantly. It had been a hot day, and one of the teachers had spotted him lying on the floor, but as it was his lunch hour they assumed he was sunbathing. I could have told them differently; John never sunbathed, he burned easily, like me, so we always sat in the shade. After a while they went over to ask if he wanted a cup of tea, and realised something was wrong, and then called an ambulance. It was very poignant that he had collapsed and died right next to the barbecue he was building with the boys.

Pablo was shocked to hear about John; so shocked that when he told his parents they invited me to go and spend a week with them in Murcia in Spain. I found that being bereaved made me feel insecure. My home was the place I felt safe in, but also it had all the memories of Anita and John, and my inclination was not to leave it.

But my children pointed out what an opportunity it was for me to have a holiday with people who regarded me as a friend. And when I thought about it, if I shut myself away from people, after a while no one would bother with me. I wasn't the first person to be bereaved, and I wouldn't be the last, but grief had made me selfish.

So I went over to Spain, and had a great week. They took me out sightseeing every day, and I was so tired that I was actually able to sleep at night. Once home I heard from Eric, who had telephoned whilst I was away. He was a French student who had come over at the age of sixteen in 1980 to stay with us; now married, with his own children. Eric and Christine had known John well, and were also shocked, as he always seemed to be so healthy. I went over and spent a long weekend with them in France, but when I came home, depression reared its ugly head.

I was lucky that Jim had sublet his flat, and moved in with me for a while. It was his choice, but I was so grateful for his company, and it meant if I wasn't there, someone was always around for Purdie. My dear Purdie had been my salvation. When I was not working, and Jim was at work, it was tempting to just stay in my bedroom all day, shut away from the world. If I met someone and they commiserated with me, I would end up in tears, but if they said nothing, then that was wrong too, I felt they didn't care. There was just no pleasing me.

John had been right about Purdie; she was my shadow, always with me, and she sat with me in my bedroom, her big eyes staring at me and her tail wagging. In the end my conscience got to me, and I did take her out, and I met people, and I learned that I just had to deal with it.

I felt like I should never laugh again, or be happy, or listen to music, so the radio remained off. This, of course, is ridiculous, as life has to go on, and when you think about it, those that have left us would want us to be happy, but such was the state of my mind at that time.

But Purdie was having none of it. She actually lifted me out of my depression, which I carefully tried to hide from my children. I don't know how she knew that she had to make me laugh, but she did. She became like a cartoon dog. She danced around in the streams whilst Jake stood barking at the side, egging her on, but not wanting to get his own feet wet. She larked around with him. Seeing them play was the funniest sight ever, little and large frisking away in front of me. Throwing a ball for her was even more hilarious. She looked most ungainly when she jumped, she didn't have the ball skills that Jake had being a collie, and although I didn't want to laugh because I felt like I was disrespecting Anita and John's memory, I couldn't help myself.

In July of 1997, I felt the need to go and visit Tom and the girls again, so I booked my ticket, which of course cost a fortune because it was during the summer holidays. But after many years of watching what I spent, I felt I no longer cared. Seeing family was worth every penny of that fare.

After we had taken out a second mortgage of sixty thousand pounds for the Florida venture, because neither John nor I liked owing money, we saved every penny that we could, and had repaid eighteen thousand pounds of that mortgage already. I also used the redundancy money I got from Crest. But when he died, because it was an endowment policy, that eighteen thousand pounds had been refunded to me. It was ironic that, for the first time in years I had spare cash, but not my John to share it with me.

When Tom came to meet me at the airport he was holding Ashley in his arms, and Becky and Katey were on either side of him. It touched my heart to see him trying to fill the impossible gap left by Anita, and although the girls hugged me in welcome, I noticed they were looking tearful. Knowing that children are much more resilient than adults, I wondered why this was, and I asked Tom later when they were in bed.

"Well they have conflicting emotions when they see you; joy because you are a link with their mother, and pain because you look and sound like her, which makes them realise how much they miss her."

Of course, my British accent, and Anita had looked just like me when I was younger; no wonder they were struggling with it. During my stay with them I was very impressed with the way Tom was coping. Ashley, who was now two years old, was beginning to get quite chatty. Her bubbly nature reminded me so much of Anita, and her sense of humour. When Tom was at work she told me: "My dad is out chasing the bad guys!"

Carol had been helping out quite a bit with babysitting, although Tom rarely went out and left them. She had been widowed quite suddenly before Anita died, which was very sad for her. Tom's dad had collapsed with a fatal heart attack, so she now lived in the house they had shared whilst bringing up the children. It was a big house to live on her own, and she was thinking of getting herself somewhere smaller, although it had obviously been useful for Tom and the girls to share after Anita died. He had now moved into a house of their own, within a short distance of Carol.

Getting the right daytime nanny had been difficult, but Tom was hopeful that the current one would stay. She took us all to the open air pool whilst Tom was at work, and we sat by the baby pool whilst Ashley happily splashed about. Becky and Katey could swim, so they went off to go in the other pool.

The weather in Greensboro at that time was very hot, and much hotter than I prefer. They all took it in their stride, being used to it. I had always visited early in the summer before, because I can't cope with extreme heat. Luckily houses and restaurants all had air conditioning, but when I was outside, I had to sit in the shade to avoid being burnt.

Jim came to meet me from the airport on my return, and I couldn't help remembering back to March, when John had met me after I had stayed on following the funeral. My son has always been a great support to me in many ways, and I believe that is because he saw John doing it, and learnt from that.

When we got home, Purdie greeted me rapturously. I knew she would have been well looked after, but we were so close, she went everywhere with me, even out in the car. I had come to rely on her a lot. Purdie kept me sane and made me laugh. She had an amazing zest for life, and being able to take her to work with me was a huge advantage. The children loved her too. Robbie, the eldest boy, used to lay on the floor with his head resting on her stomach watching TV. I knew he loved her, and she was always so gentle with the children.

I had recently met another nanny named Lesley, who looked after two little girls from a family that were the best friends of Chris and Ian. During the holidays we took the children out together; they had fun, and it was nice to have someone to talk to whilst they played. Lesley was to become a loyal and close friend, and although I don't see her that often, that friendship has endured for twenty-two years.

During August bank holiday that year I popped down to visit my dad and Betty and Ron at Herne Bay. I was sleeping in the lounge, and when I woke up, I put the TV on to hear the news. It was a huge shock to hear that Princess Diana had been killed in a car crash in Paris. I immediately thought about her boys, just in their teens, having to grow up without their mother, and my heart broke for them. That situation was so familiar, and when I saw them later walking behind the car at her funeral, it was heartbreaking, but their courage was truly inspirational. 1997 was a bad year!

Chapter Twenty-one

I was very relieved to leave 1997 behind, and embrace 1998. So many sad and unexpected deaths in one year. Because Phil is non verbal, I have no idea if he understood that Anita and John had died. He had not seen Anita for a while since she had moved to America, and now he was living at Hastings, he only saw us once a month.

During that year there were get togethers for people who had worked at Crest, and I offered to host one at my house. We were all missing being at the shops, and it was great to meet up with my old comrades again, and have a glass of wine and a chat.

I had such happy memories of my years at Crest, I felt like I wanted to recapture them; not that you ever can, because nothing ever stays the same. I was friendly with Sue, who had been the manager of our Orpington branch, and she was now working for Royal Doulton, a shop within the Debenhams store. She was looking for someone to work ten hours a week, so I decided to do five hours on Monday and five on Saturday. I just wanted to get back into shop work because I had enjoyed it so much in the past.

I worked there for a year, but it was nothing like Crest. I worked on my own, and we didn't have many customers. Sue took her time off and I was her relief assistant, but after being used to having a manager's job, I didn't find it challenging enough, so I left in 1999. The best part of it had been the generous discount against anything I bought from the store.

There was another sad death in the family before the year 2000 arrived. John's brother Malcolm passed away in his late fifties of

Anita on the right with her best friend Linda, 1986.

Carol on a Rose Crest outing, Christmas 1986.

Anita and Andrea, 1987.

Anita and Tom, 1988.

Family photograph, 1988.
Betty, Dad, Carol, Anita, Ron, Doreen, Andrea, Jim and Phil.

Carol's visit to Anita's family in America, 1996.

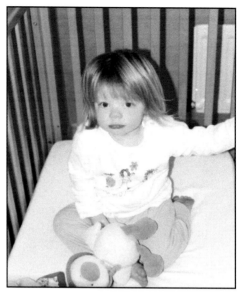

Imogen, 2000.

Becky, Katey and Ashley, 2000.

Becky's wedding in 2013. From left: Carol, Keith, Ashley, Tom, Becky, Nate, Katey, Carol B and Mick.

Jim, Carol and Andrea, 2016.

Keith and Carol, 2018.

Rosie and Natty, Carol's great-grandchildren, 2019.

Andrea and David, 2019.

Imogen and Andrea, 2019.

Carol behind her bookstall at Southport.

the same lung disease that had claimed his mother's life. Andrea, Andrew and I went to his funeral, and went back to the house afterwards to support Editha, who was devastated at his loss.

In the summer of 1999 Andrea told me she was pregnant, the baby was due in February 2000. I was as excited as Andrew and Andrea were; a new life coming into the world, another grandchild, and this one was in England, so I could play a much bigger part in its life.

I had now worked for Chris for four years. Michael was now at school, just like the others, so I took the children and dropped them off at their three different schools, then walked Jake and Purdie. After that I did some ironing, and before long it was time to go and meet them all from school. During holiday time it was quite hectic, but we usually went out somewhere with Lesley and the two girls that she looked after. Lesley had been a tower of strength to me at times when I felt low. She encouraged me to go to church, which I did for a while, and then a lady from the church came round to the house to chat to me, she had also lost her husband, so she knew how I felt, and I found talking to her really helped.

I have always felt the presence of both Anita and John at times since they passed away. When Andrea went into labour, she was taken to hospital, and was in labour for a good few hours. Andrew didn't want to leave her, so he could not phone me, and it was late at night, and everything seems so much worse at night. I was pacing around so anxiously; my baby was giving birth to her own baby, and I was so worried about her. I went through the motions of going to bed, but didn't expect to sleep, and kept the phone right next to me.

The next thing that I could remember was seeing Anita. She had a long white dress on, standing at the foot of my bed, holding her arms out to me with such a peaceful look on her face.

"Don't worry about Andrea, Mum, I won't let anything happen to her, she will be fine," she said.

I found that very comforting, and within a few hours I got the message that Andrea had given birth to a beautiful baby girl.

She was named Imogen Anita, and became my youngest granddaughter. Her birth felt so uplifting to me; proof that life does go on. She has always been a beautiful girl, both inside and out, and I have been privileged to be able to see her grow up to a

g

lovely young woman. Being a part of her life, and looking after her, has always been a pleasure.

When I have told people about my experience of seeing Anita just before Imogen's birth, they have been of the opinion that I was dreaming, but I truly believe she was there. My girls were so close, in fact all my children have been close to one another, it makes sense that Anita would have been watching over her, and would want to reassure me that Andrea would be OK.

In her early years, Imogen looked like Andrea, who in turn looked like her dad, which made her feel even more precious. It is such a shame he never got to see his granddaughter. He would have been so proud of her. The most exciting part of entering the new millenium for me, was the birth of Imogen. Andrea has proved to be a very caring mother, taking her duties very seriously.

It was now three years since we had lost John and Anita. I had used the money that came to me to have a new kitchen, add a conservatory, and decorate right through the house. I had foolishly imagined if I gave the house a new look, it would help me to move on. But the window in Anita's old bedroom still bore traces of the Speedo sticker she had attached there one day, and at the time I had scolded her about it. Now I couldn't bear to take it off.

John's armchair still stood in the lounge, empty, and I still expected to see his car pull into the drive at night. Several of my friends had told me I was far too young to spend the rest of my life on my own, and they suggested that I join a club, but I had resisted all their attempts to encourage me. There was no point, because I felt I had enough happy memories to last me for the rest of my life.

My dad was now ninety-one, and sadly I could see he was declining. He was losing his sight, so he had to give up driving. He had always been a very independent man, and he played down his lack of sight, because it really worried Betty, but I had noticed him feeling for his cup when she brought his tea in.

I bought myself a caravan on a site near to them, and with Purdie I went down for the weekends. I would go round and spend the day with them, then go back to the caravan at night. I never felt on my own with Purdie, she was such a great companion. Dad said I could have stayed with them, there was no need to buy a caravan, but I enjoyed having my own space to go back to. I have always been an independent person.

I really looked forward to those weekends at Herne Bay, and I was able to take my dad out in the car for rides. One day he expressed a wish to go to Broadstairs. It was a lovely sunny day, so I took him and Betty there, and he walked down onto the sandy beach and sat on a bench for a while. I knew he couldn't see much, but he was very contented; he never complained about anything. We walked into a local restaurant to have dinner, and, bless him, he fell asleep right afterwards, and we had to wake him up to get him back into the car. I realised he didn't have many more years left, and I felt the need to be close to him. It would actually do me good to put some energy into helping him. Betty didn't drive, so he was stuck at home, and additionally I had promised both my mum and dad in the past that I would always keep an eye on Ron, and support him, so the simple solution was to move to Herne Bay.

Chapter Twenty-two

I had always loved going to Herne Bay. That part of the Kent coast boasted of the best weather in the UK with very little rainfall. I had spent holidays there as a child when my dad built the bungalow at Studd Hill, but that had been sold when he lost his business. Luckily at a later date, my mum and dad were able to retire there, and my mum had spent six years enjoying her trips to whist drives, and enjoying the nice clean sea air.

During the years when they were growing up, we were frequent visitors with the children, and when Becky, Katey and Ashley came along, Anita and Tom made the journey over to England, and were able to show my dad his great-granddaughters. This was the last time my dad saw Anita, as it was just over a year before she passed away.

When I told Jim and Andrea I was thinking of moving to Herne Bay, their reaction was very positive. Jim was thinking of going back to his own flat, as the nurse renting it was moving on somewhere else, so he said I didn't need to worry about him. Andrea, who was living at Walderslade at the time, pointed out that the journey was about the same as it was already, but in the opposite direction, and it would be nice to visit me at the coast.

I went to see an estate agent, who came round and valued the house. I had never bought or sold a house before, or actually dealt with estate agents, John had done all that, so I had to trust the agent. To my great surprise, somebody viewed it on the first day and offered me the full asking price. This was surprising, after the struggles we had some ten years earlier to even get viewings.

I wondered if it had been under priced, but it was too late, and solicitors had now become involved on both sides. I realised I would have about three months to find somewhere to live. Fortunately I still had the caravan, and summer was fast approaching, so if necessary I could use that if I had to until I found somewhere.

The upper part of Herne Bay has a village called Beltinge, it was at that time a quiet little village, surrounded by fields which housed caravans, some very old and disused, but at the end of the village, just off the main road, an estate of houses had been built. They had been built in old fashioned cottage style to be in keeping with the area, and they had neat little gardens as well. I found one I liked. It was spacious, which was ideal as my family would be visiting, and I made an offer, which was accepted.

The good thing about moving to Herne Bay at that time was I could get more for my money. That no longer applies, as the popularity of Herne Bay and Whitstable has shot up thanks to Londoners coming down to the Kent coast to buy holiday homes.

I swapped a four bedroomed semi-detached house at Coney Hall, for a four bedroomed detached house at Herne Bay, and I made a profit, which meant I would be financially secure for the rest of my life if I was careful.

As time went on, my sale was going through very quickly and the new owners were anxious to move in immediately, but the sellers of the house I had chosen were taking their time in finding what they wanted. The whole situation was becoming very stressful, so when an advertisement for another house popped through the door, I went and viewed it.

This was also a modern house, in the little hamlet known as Bishopstone, which was just beyond Beltinge. The house was in a road that had a mixture of new properties with nicely laid out front gardens and paths, and then bungalows along the road, with a gate at the end which led into Bishopstone Glen, which was a beautiful place to walk.

The house that I viewed was on the end, and it had conifers at the front and in the back garden, which afforded me privacy from anyone walking down the road. I fell in love with that house immediately, and I knew my Purdie, Charley, and I would be happy there.

Just before I moved into the house, I popped round to see my dad and Betty to update them about the progress, and when I could expect to move in. Betty was very excited, she said there was a really nice builder next door, and he had come round to ask if they could borrow some electricity whilst they were building a bungalow, and he would reimburse them for the costs. I wasn't greatly interested about that; but later, when I went back to the caravan, I spotted two men working next door.

During the long weekend that I was there, she kept on talking about this nice man and I knew what she was doing, she was trying to pair me off with someone, and I wasn't having any of it. If the man was that nice, he would be spoken for. Most men in their fifties would have a partner or wife, and I had absolutely no desire to get involved with anyone again, and I told her so.

On Sunday when I came round to see them again, suddenly a face popped up from behind the fence. "Oh, what a lovely dog," said a man, who had a very friendly smiling face. He was making a big fuss of Purdie, and of course she was lapping it all up. My attitude towards him softened; if he liked animals he must be nice, so we stood talking about all the great walks there were around that area.

By the way he was addressing me, I could tell that Betty had told him quite a lot about me. He asked if the sale was going through smoothly, and I said hopefully it was. He had really taken a liking to Purdie and he asked me if he could come out for a walk with her next time I went. He explained that they didn't usually work on Sundays, but now they were anxious to get the bungalow finished, so they were working every day. I agreed to let him come out with me, as he clearly liked Purdie a lot.

The day I moved from Birch Tree Avenue was a painful one, even though I had thought it was the best thing for me. So many memories were stored within that house, most of them really happy ones, and our dear Prince was buried in the garden. I had sold most of the furniture except the beds, as I was planning to buy light wood furniture as the new house was a modern one.

I had Purdie and Charley in the car with me. Charley was protesting furiously at the indignity of being in a cat carrier. She had always lived at one house, and was twelve years old. The only time I used the carrier was when she went to the vet for her yearly booster.

The key was not being released until two o'clock, so I gave

150

Charley some food, and she then went to sleep. I took Purdie for a walk around the glen, which was just yards from the house, and another five minutes away from there was the beach.

When I returned to the car, the sun was shining very brightly. It was the last day of May 2000, and it felt like summer already. At two o'clock I knocked on the front door, and the outgoing man gave me the keys, explained how everything worked, and then wished me well.

Suddenly I was alone, and I had a wobble. Was I mad to move to a completely new area with people I didn't know, and leave all the comforting familiarity of Coney Hall behind me? But a new life had been my reason for moving, a chance to make a fresh start and rebuild my life.

There was a ring at the doorbell and I went to answer it, Purdie at my heels. On my doorstep stood a man with a friendly face wreathed in smiles.

"Hi, I am Martin, I live next door with Anna. Welcome to Bishopstone. If there is anything you want, just let us know."

"That's very kind of you. I am fine, the removal men will be here soon; everything is under control."

"Don't forget now; just ring our doorbell, we are here for you." He then made a big fuss of Purdie who had decided he was a friendly visitor.

After he had gone, I had a warm glow inside me. I had friendly caring neighbours. Maybe someone had told him I was on my own, but he had certainly helped me over my wobble. The doorbell went again, and this time it was my brother Ron. He had come round to help me unpack the smaller but very necessary items; mainly things like the kettle, frying pan, and mugs for the kitchen.

By the end of the afternoon the beds had all been unloaded and made up, the three piece suite was in place, and it was looking a bit more like home. I had to buy a new table and chairs and lounge furniture, but all the bedrooms had built-in wardrobes. I was looking forward to going to the shops to choose new furniture; everything we owned in the past had been second hand.

Later we took Purdie for a walk along the beach. The tide was out and the sun was still shining. It was a perfect evening. We bought fish and chips from the local shop in Beltinge, and sat on the cliff top to eat them. If this was a taste of my new life, I could get used it.

Chris had been worried that I might leave her, but I had worked out a plan I thought might work. I would travel up to Chislehurst on a Tuesday morning; it took about an hour by car, and I started work at eight o'clock. At the end of the day I would go to Jim's flat and stay there. I would also stay there after work on Wednesday, and then go back to Herne Bay after work on Thursday. I finished earlier on Thursdays as Chris was home by four o'clock. Not only would it save me petrol and time travelling back and forth, but also it gave me the opportunity to see Jim.

The builder, whose name was Keith Taylor, came round, and we walked Purdie to Reculver. He knew lots of local places to walk; one of them was at a local country area called Grove Ferry, where the river widened out into a lake with a nice walk around it.

I did wonder if Purdie would be jealous of Keith, as for a few years now, it had been just me and her, but she was fine with him. I have always said he is like the pied piper, and so was John. Animals just seem to be drawn to certain people.

One way of describing my Purdie was that she was a big puff of wind. She looked big and bold, but you could see she was all mouth and trousers. This time she was larking around in the water as usual, and then she saw a swan gliding peacefully along. Because she wanted to show off to Keith she swam after it, chasing it, and I was hopping about all worried that she might frighten it. But I needn't have worried. When we rounded the next bend, it was to see Purdie frantically swimming back towards us, pursued by a very angry swan. Keith and I just couldn't stop laughing at the spectacle.

And she never seemed to learn from her misfortunes. Another day we were walking along the clifftop path, which stretches from Bishopstone into Herne Bay, and behind the path are gardens with sheds in them. Up on one shed was a cat stretched out luxuriously, enjoying the sun. Purdie leapt forward barking, something she would not have dreamt of doing to Charley. The cat was having none of it. He stood up, showing he was a big cat, and jumped off the shed roof, heading straight for Purdie, who blinked with astonishment to see the size of him, and when she realised he was coming for her, turned and ran away, yelping at the same time at the thought of what he might do to her.

The lady who lived in the house, hearing all the noise, put her head over the fence and explained that she had two dogs as well, but the cat wore the trousers, and kept them in their place. By then the cat had decided Purdie wasn't worth worrying about, and he stalked off swishing his tail.

Keith and I had by now formed a solid friendship. I had told him about Phil, and how he regularly came for the weekend, because I knew that if he could not cope with the knowledge that I had a son with many difficulties, then our friendship would not last. But he wasn't fazed by it. He met Phil, and I knew my son liked him, as he put his head up and smiled, which he doesn't do to everyone.

My dad liked him, and he had already charmed Betty, so then I introduced him to Jim and Andrea, who were a little bit cautious about him, not knowing what to expect. But they did not need to worry; I was quite happy to have a good friend and companion to share outings and holidays with.

I had been travelling up to work for Chris from Herne Bay for a year, and the children were getting older. She told me that she only needed me during holiday times now. I didn't really like being away from my home for three days a week, and when I returned, the weekends seemed to pass so quickly. So I decided it was time to leave. I knew I could get work locally through a nanny agency, so I explained all this to Chris, who understood, and I left.

Keith had just finished building another bungalow, and he wanted to take a holiday in America. He wanted to go for a month, hire a car, and tour. I had been to America every year since Becky was born, even after John died, and if I went with Keith, we could drive to Greensboro, meet Tom and the girls and spend some time with them.

So I took a month off too, and we had a holiday to remember. We visited so many places. We went down south, had a trip on a Mississippi Paddle Steamer, and visited Gracelands, the home of Elvis Presley. We stayed at many motels in different areas, and most of them had open air swimming pools which we made good use of.

During the last week, we travelled to Greensboro to visit Tom and the girls. They took to him immediately because Keith is a joker; he mimics accents, and he had the girls in stitches. We did lots of fun things with them like riding go-carts and visiting Wet and Wild, where Keith took them down the very high chute that I am afraid I couldn't go on because of my fear of heights. We were also regular visitors to MacDonalds, and the local cinema, as well as going bowling. We packed so much into that week. It was now four years since the death of Anita, and I had nothing but admiration for the way Tom was bringing the girls up. They were becoming very independent and responsible young ladies.

Although I had a great holiday, I had missed Purdie; a month was a long time to be parted from her. Luckily Andrew's dad and his wife were visiting from Australia, so they had stayed at my house and looked after Purdie. When we saw her, she greeted us excitedly, and Charley appeared too, leaving the garden to venture into the kitchen and show her face.

I went back to work with a local nanny agency, and did various temporary jobs for local families. This suited me very well at the time. One family that I worked for owned a farm shop business and grew all their own fruit and vegetables. They invited me to help myself to raspberries, strawberries and cabbages, as well as other produce they were growing. They had two delightful children that I took to Dreamland in Margate, and I was very sorry when that temporary job came to an end.

In the winter of 2001, my dad developed flu. He was now ninety-two, and as a precaution, his doctor had arranged for him to go into hospital. I took Betty and Ron to visit him regularly, and he slowly seemed to be getting better. We were all hoping he would come home soon, but we had to be patient. At his age, his recovery wasn't going to be swift.

Chapter Twenty-three

In January 2002, my dad was moved into the local hospital at Herne Bay as he was recovering well. It was a lot easier to get there to visit him, with plenty of parking on site. He was so looking forward to coming home, and we too wanted him back safely. At almost ninety-three, he was still as sharp as ever in his mind, and he was missing his armchair and his dog second only to Betty and his home.

I was sad when it was announced that Princess Margaret had died, aged seventy. The Royal Family are noted for being a long living family, indeed The Queen Mother survived the death of her daughter by a month, and she also passed away on the 30th March that same year aged one hundred and one.

My dad was allowed to come home in late March, but his needs had increased, so carers came in. Betty was trying her best to care for him, but it was hard for her, so it was suggested that my dad would go into respite care for a couple of weeks. He was put into a local care home, and during that time it was his ninety-third birthday. They made a special cake for him and we all went along for his birthday celebrations. I remember saying to him: "You are doing well Dad, a few more years, and you'll be a hundred."

Sadly that was not to be. Two days before he was due home, the care home rang me to say he had passed away that morning. We were all devastated, and I tried to help Betty as much as I could with all the necessary arrangements that go on afterwards, remembering just how fragile I had felt when it happened to me.

When the post mortem was carried out they found he had cancer of the pancreas. He was about three months into the disease, and the coroner told me that it was a blessing in disguise, as the next three months would have been the time when he would have been in great pain. Although I would miss him so much, I thanked God he had not suffered, and had led a long and happy life.

We helped Betty to sell her bungalow, as it needed a lot of decorating and was too big for her, so we moved her to a smaller one. The owner of this one had decorated it all up ready for selling. Ron had decided he wanted to be independent now, so had bought himself a mobile home which he occupied during summer months, and then during the four months that the site was closed he stayed with Betty.

In 2002 a new programme called Pop Idol was aired on TV. Keith used to come over at the weekend, and we didn't watch it, thinking it would be something that would appeal more to teenagers. By chance, on the penultimate week of the programme, whilst Phil was staying with us, I switched on the TV, and Phil smiled when he heard *Yesterday* being sung. Keith, who was in another room, called out exactly what I was thinking.

"Well, whoever that is has an amazing voice!"

The singer was Gareth Gates. I was immediately drawn to this spiky haired youngster, who had the voice of an angel, but such a bad stammer that it was hard for him even to say his name. What courage he had to stand up there in front of the nation, knowing that he would be interviewed afterwards!

We did vote for him, but Will Young was the winner. However, they were both given a recording contract, and went on to have lucrative careers. I have followed Gareth's career and met him several times, and he continues to inspire me. In later years, Debs, who was a moderator on his official website, became my friend. She set up her own website and invited me to be a moderator. It has been my pleasure to help her run it, and in return she has helped me with my own website and Youtube channel, as well as other social media.

By the time 2003 had arrived, after I had spent three years in my house, Keith and I decided to live together. He had proved to be a dear friend and companion, so it made sense to both of us to share our lives together. I sold my house and he sold his bungalow at Birchington, so we put our money together and bought a thatched cottage at West Stourmouth.

The cottage was set in almost an acre of ground, and had a swimming pool, which was well used in the summer. The house itself was big, with several bedrooms and en-suites, and we both loved the experience of living in a grade two listed cottage. We had some great pool parties whilst we were there; the family came over, and some of our neighbours, and we enjoyed that lifestyle.

At Christmas 2003, Tom and the girls came over from America to stay with us. It was lovely to have them with us at Christmas; there were lots of fun things going on, and then they went to spend New Year with Mick and Joan before flying home.

2004 arrived, and during that year Purdie, who was now ten years old, developed a cough. Unfortunately, when visiting the vet, he found she had heart disease, so she had to have some pills to help her. We managed to keep her going until August 2005, then we had to make that decision; we could tell she had had enough, so we had to let her go. I was devastated, because it was my Purdie who had helped me to pick up my life again back in 1997. I could never forget her faithfulness and loyalty.

But we didn't last long without a dog. We decided that this time we would have a puppy, and not rescue a dog, so when I heard there was a litter of golden retriever puppies at West Malling, I went to see the breeder. She said they would be ready in a couple of weeks, so Keith and I dutifully returned later. There were nine little fluffy golden puppies, all vying for their mother's attention. The breeder invited us to pick them up and choose the one we wanted. How could you choose one from all those cuddly little bundles? It's not easy. I picked up several and held them, but there was only one that really moulded itself into my arms. The others either wriggled or trembled, but this pup promptly fell asleep in my arms.

So it looked like he had chosen us himself. He slept in my arms on the way home, and seemed quite content. We named him Leo. He was a calm dog, but never really bonded with other dogs. We found out why; he was the smallest of the litter and had been pushed out by his siblings when food was served. But apart from that, he was a lovely family boy, and as Imogen was now five

157

years old, he was the ideal dog to have as a family pet; he was so gentle with her.

Now that Imogen had started school, it was a good opportunity for Andrea to return to work. She went for an interview at a special school, and was initially employed as a teaching assistant.

After a short period of time it became apparent that she had great rapport with the students, and she was asked to do individual work that was more emotionally focused. To enhance this work she asked if she could do specific learning, and then started counselling/therapeutic training.

She had previously also done an Open University Course. As I have stated before, sometimes exams come at a time when you just can't take them for one reason or another, so to be able to take them as an adult is definitely uplifting; it means we are never too old to learn.

It was not an easy job, and she had my admiration for taking it on. A lot of the children came from homes where they were just not understood; they had special needs, but not all parents can cope with that. So the help and support that she gave was invaluable. I asked her one night why she had chosen that profession, as she had been surrounded by it all her life.

"But that is why, Mum, I wanted to do something to help them."

I am sure her contribution was gratefully accepted, and she was very good at her job; full of empathy, but also determined to help the children in her care. She has the same caring nature as her father.

It is different when you have your own child with special needs. It's a natural thing for a mother to fight to get everything that child needs, and to make their life more comfortable. Anyone else would have done what I did. But when it comes to helping other children with special needs and working alongside them, it takes a special person to do that, and I am proud of Andrea for this very reason. All my energy was spent helping Phil, but I don't think I could have coped with a job that involved the challenges that present themselves in a special needs school. She proved to be a very valuable asset to the school; managing to get children to trust in her and confide their worries, which can be a daunting task, especially with children who have autism.

Another notable event for me during this year was that we

bought ourselves a computer. I have to admit that technology scares me a bit, especially when I have to ask a ten year old to help me with my mobile phone. But Keith and I both realised we were getting left behind. Not only could you surf the net, but whenever we went shopping, and we ordered something, we were asked for our email address. Everybody seemed to have a computer.

It was that year my next book, a novel, entitled *Not Just an Affair*, was written. I had valiantly typed it out on a word processor, but the file had to be converted, and it made life a lot more difficult. I realised that if I did write any more books, it would be a lot easier to do it on the computer, and just use a floppy disk.

So I mastered the computer enough to use it to store my writing on, but I think if I lived to be one hundred, I would still have a lot to learn. It's such a good idea that children learn from a young age, and by the time they get to school, most of them know how to use an Apple ipad. Indeed, young children often seem to opt for watching something on Netflix on an ipad or other computer tablet, rather than on the TV these days.

Another happy event in 2005 was the marriage of Prince Charles, Prince of Wales, to Camilla Parker Bowles on 8th April. Since the death of Diana in 1997, Camilla had been his constant companion. She had remained dignified when vilified by the press and others as 'the other woman' in his marriage to Diana. Her loyalty and stability whilst all this was going on was just what Charles needed, and it must have been wonderful for them both to finally marry and spend the rest of their lives together.

I think it's wrong for people to judge, because nobody knows what goes on behind closed doors. As I have stated before, I feel as if I have known Charles all my life, as I grew up at the same time as him, and the Royal Family have always been of great interest to me.

We are lucky to have a Royal Family, and sometimes they don't get the respect they deserve for doing a very difficult job. Our lovely Queen is a symbol of stability, for she has given her life to ruling this country, and it makes me proud to be British. Many other countries, especially America, would love to have their own Royal Family; this is why they have such a fascination with ours.

My parents were also royalists like me, and I grew up with a sense of pride in the monarchy. Times have changed now, but I still hold the same respect for the job they do; the never ending public appearances they make, the number of handshakes in a day; and now the press put their private lives under scrutiny, which is not right. It didn't happen years ago, but that is the way of life now for everyone.

Chapter Twenty-four

Early in 2006, we decided to sell the cottage. We had spent three great years there, but the running costs were high. We had to maintain the swimming pool, keep the weeds in the garden under control, and then the house itself was big, so cleaning it took a long time. Reflecting now, when you live in a property of that size, you need a gardener, a house cleaner and a pool cleaner, but we were both still working just to maintain it all.

We had assumed we would get a buyer quite quickly, but a thatched cottage is not for everyone. We had a visit from Kirstie Allsopp, because they wanted to feature it on 'Location, Location, Location'. Channel 4 had seen our cottage advertised on the estate agents website and had chosen it, plus three other properties, to use on the programme.

But even with the television coverage, we still didn't sell it, and it became a never ending task getting the house in pristine condition for all the viewings. Some of the feedback was amazing. It was advertised as a grade two listed cottage, so we were surprised when one couple viewing complained that it was "Too cottagey." Another couple said the garden was too big and they didn't like gardening, even though the size of the garden was listed on the details. Keith referred to them afterwards as "The Grislets from Chislett."

Then after about six months, a couple came along; it was June now, the garden was a riot of colour, and it all looked really nice. The swimming pool was uncovered and it sparkled with the sun shining on it. They fell in love with it, just as we had three years earlier. They were adamant that they wanted it and made an offer, which we accepted.

My dream had always been to design my own house and have it built for me. John and I had spoken about it in the past; everyone is entitled to have their own dream, and he had wanted to build it for us.

Well it hadn't happened then, because circumstances had denied us that. But now suddenly I was seeing land available on a plot very close to the sea. Of course, it was going to take several months for the sale of our cottage to go through, but we had already decided that we needed less spacious accommodation, and as we had both sold a house to buy the cottage, we were going to revert back to having a house each.

Keith had lots of contacts in the building trade after building his own houses, so together we sat down and designed a house that was just average in size, but big enough to accommodate my family when they came to stay. I was very excited, as I now knew my dream was going to be realised.

It was a challenging task for Keith, as the plot was set on sloping ground, which was clay, and very close to the sea. It would be against the backdrop of Bishopstone Glen; I knew it was the perfect place to build a house. To be able to plan the size of the rooms was something really special, I was so lucky.

It took several months to build, and we had our fair share of bad weather at that time. I remember that there were wooden boards leading to the front of the house to avoid getting stuck in the mud. Little Charley cat was now nineteen years old, and I used to watch her with great trepidation as she made her way down the garden, skilfully missing falling into any of the holes. She had by now lost most of her sight, but still opted to go outside, so it was even more remarkable.

We spent a few months living with Keith's mother whilst we were waiting for the house to be habitable. She opened up her bungalow to us, and Leo and Charley, which was very kind. It's often quite difficult to find somewhere to rent when you have animals.

Not Just an Affair was published in 2006 to my delight. I now had two books to my name. I had realised whilst writing it, that it's good for me to have a focus in my life, and writing is something that takes me away from everyday living. I enjoy inventing my characters and plots, and I don't think I would be complete as a person if I didn't write something every day. It's my escapism, a place where I can use my imagination, and I always try to write from the heart; sincerity is most important.

In 2006 I took up a new hobby. When I was in the local library I saw advertised that players were wanted for a local badminton club. John and I had played briefly back in the eighties, but I hadn't done it since. When I phoned the man to ask if I could join (I am laughing now as I write this), I told him I was sixty-two, and hoped it wasn't too old to join.

He explained that most of the players were older people, so that was fine. But I only went a couple of times; obviously I was a bit rusty, and I had no idea how competitive this club was. One man told me off, because he said when I played with him I had lost him the game, but when I played against him, with another partner, I had played much better. My day was saved as there were several people there from another club, their hall was out of order that week, but they invited me to join their non-competitive club on the following week.

Thirteen years later I am still there, and I have improved, and what a great crowd they are. I would recommend something like that to anyone who may have been bereaved, or moved to a new area, it's a great way to meet new friends. If anyone had told me I would still be playing badminton at seventy-five I would have laughed at them, so there you go! I hasten to add that Keith came for a little while, but decided he preferred to sit down in the evening after a busy day. I have always been the sort of person who can't sit down for long unless I am writing, so sport is really good for me. We have seen quite a few different players come and go from our club since I joined, but there are the stalwarts, who even started before me, and to their credit Herne Badminton Club has been going now for about forty years with some of the original players still there.

Before we knew it 2007 was here, but the house was still not ready to be occupied. I was longing to get in there, especially when Christmas approached, as the family always come to stay with me, and Christmas would not be the same without them.

Because it was so close to Christmas, and the weather was so cold, all the builders had packed up that year; even the man who fitted the doors had stopped. But I was determined nothing would stop me from celebrating Christmas in the new house, so Keith finally agreed. We hung sheets where the doors would be, and found an old carpet to put on the lounge floor over the wooden floorboards. The kitchen was installed, so I would be able to cook Christmas dinner, and we had to put temporary curtains up at all the windows.

I guess this must all sound very horrifying, as though we were living like gypsies, but having my family with me was the most important thing to me, so I didn't care, and we had a lovely Christmas as usual.

As soon as the New Year of 2008 dawned, all the traders returned, and together with Keith helping, the doors were hung, the rooms decorated, curtains were bought and fitted, and carpets laid. It was lovely to finally get the house as we wanted, but as regards the garden, that took a good few months to sort out. Because it was a sloping site, the back garden had to be specially designed, with steps leading down to the lawn area with banks on each side. Keith put a gate there to stop Leo from going on the lawn, as he would have dug right down to Australia if we let him. He had his own patio and gravel area all around the house, where he loved to lay out in the sun. That is also where we have always had our barbecues.

The house is set back from the road as it widens out, so we have quite a large front garden with a winding path to the front door. The garage is set to the side of it, and we laughed one day, as because our house is next to Reculver Country Park, we had to adhere to certain regulations, and the garage had to be constructed to look exactly the same as the house; in short, a smaller cottage with pebble-dash. When our new telephone book was delivered, one was put in our outside mailbox, and another one was put outside the side door of the garage, because whoever delivered it must have thought they were two houses. If they had approached the front of the garage they would have seen the up and over door.

Keith has always been a huge fan of formula one racing. Sometimes he would be sitting in the lounge on a lovely sunny day with the curtains drawn, watching it. I had never really taken an interest in it, thinking just the sound of the cars buzzing round the track was irritating, so I usually did something else and left him to it. But one particular day in the winter, he was watching as usual, and from what I could gather, this race in Brazil would decide who won the championship. I just happened to glance at the screen, and to my amazement, I saw this young man overtake a car on the last corner, as apparently he only needed to come fifth to snatch the championship away from Felipe Massa. And when I took more notice, and saw the joyous celebrations, I found out his name was Lewis Hamilton, and he was British.

I will support anyone British in any sport, because I think we are such a great country; but obviously they don't always win. I was immediately drawn to this young man with so much spirit and determination. It was his first championship and he was only twenty-three. I could see then he was something special; it shone out of him, and I was convinced that he would go on and win more championships in the future. His greatest honour, he said, was being awarded an MBE by Queen Elizabeth 2nd.

Chapter Twenty-five

We had another sad event in 2009, when our little Charley cat died. She had been having pills for her kidneys for a couple of years, and lost her sight and her hearing, but never her spirit. She had never been a lap cat, being half feral, but during those last two years she became very loving, and I will always treasure that memory.

It was summertime and we had a barbecue, and had cooked some salmon as well. Imogen liked salmon, but there was some left. Charley was brushing round my legs, so I gave her some; she had always loved salmon. On that day she was very sociable, doing the rounds, brushing herself up against everybody.

But the next day, when everyone had gone home, she was restless. Next door found her stretched out in the hedge, but not happily. She seemed to be hiding herself away, so we brought her back. Then she climbed into Leo's big bed, and she didn't move and she didn't want any food.

Keith took her to the vet as I was working, and when I returned home it was to find that the vet had said it was her time, and we couldn't let her suffer. Although we missed her greatly, she had become frail, so it was the best thing for her. Our remarkable little cat had enjoyed a wonderful life, and had lasted until she was twenty-one years old.

I was by now indulging my hobby of writing about anything and everything. I joined an online writing site, and I think to date I have written about six hundred short stories. I also wrote articles about autism. It is now regarded as an interesting subject, and I have had lots of positive comments about these articles, which are meant to help and support people.

In the summer of 2009 we had a house warming party, and many of our friends came as well as family. It was a hot sunny day, so some of the visitors took advantage of that by having a dip in the sea. Our house is a very short walk from the beach; just through the glen, and then down the slope, and you are there. As soon as the weather warms up in summer I like to swim in the sea, it's better than any swimming pool, but on that particular day I couldn't as there were many people to chat to and things to be done. We had now been in our house for just over a year. I have always loved living at Herne Bay, but obviously enjoy visiting other parts of Great Britain. One particular place Keith really likes is Suffolk. The weather is very similar to our south eastern corner, which is an advantage, and he suggested that if he bought a holiday home there, he could let it out some of the time and we could use it ourselves as well.

So we started travelling to Suffolk and staying at bed and breakfast places whilst we searched for a suitable holiday home. It was amazing how nice a photograph of a house can look on a print-out from estate agent details, but when you actually go and look at it, it doesn't quite match up. We were beginning to get despondent. We thought it was quite simple, we just wanted a two bedroomed house or bungalow, with a small garden and somewhere to park the car.

Eventually we found a bungalow that was being built in the village of Westhorpe, which is near to Stowmarket. We realised we would have to wait a while for it to be finished, but the builder was so delighted that we wanted it, he agreed to reduce the price if Keith would finish the garden. This suited Keith very much, as he had his own ideas about the design of it. Westhorpe's claim to fame is that Henry VIII's sister Mary lived and died there. Her body is buried at Bury St Edmunds, but the building in which she lived, which is called Westhorpe Hall, has now become a care home.

Ever since Eileen had left Crest in 1980, we had periodically visited her at her cottage in Devon. She was now in her eighties and her health was declining. Her husband Alan had died not long after John, and her only son lived a long way away, but visited her as often as he could.

Now that it was hard for her to care for herself, she realised she would have to go into a care home, so she wrote and told me where she was. I felt so sad for her, as until her health had declined, Eileen had walked miles with her dog, and always kept herself very fit. She was now in a wheelchair, and her heart was weak. I was very anxious to go and visit her, so we booked a weekend at a bed and breakfast in Dorset, and then drove to where her care home was.

When I saw her, sitting in her wheelchair waiting to see us, I was amazed to see how happy she looked. Her body might now be frail, but she had lost none of her sense of humour and spirit. Her attitude was truly amazing; she had a right to moan about her lot, but she didn't. She had been reading a book which had amused her, and she shared some of the humour in it with us.

She asked after Leo, and we explained he was just outside in the car, in a shady spot.

"Don't leave him out there, bring him in!"

"Are you sure they won't mind?" I said doubtfully.

"Very sure, we often have visits from dogs."

So we went outside and got him. I think care homes were beginning to realise the value of dogs for people who don't feel very well. Stroking a dog can be very therapeutic, and Leo particularly, being a retriever, was very laid back. He was delighted to be brought in, and the look of happiness on Eileen's face was truly uplifting. She had never been without a dog; springer spaniels were the breed that she had always gone for in the past, but she loved all dogs.

She hadn't fancied her ham sandwiches earlier, so she fed them to Leo and he wolfed them down. Seeing her interaction with him was rewarding, and when we left her, she told us how much she had enjoyed our visit and appreciated how far we had come to see her. I felt it was the least I could have done, as when I first worked at Crest, Eileen had been so supportive, especially when I was struggling to cope. She had been a great friend to me.

In 2010, sadly, Keith's mother's health deteriorated. She had done so well living independently in her bungalow, but she was now ninety years old, and could not be left on her own any more. We found her a nice care home very near to us in Herne Bay, so we were able to visit her frequently.

It is never nice to see your loved one ageing, but the relief we felt that she was being looked after so well was immeasurable. We had wondered if we could care for her ourselves, but our house wasn't really big enough, although fortunately we were able to bring her home to spend some time with us that Christmas.

Keith's brother and his wife lived in Worcestershire, so they couldn't visit that often. We were lucky that it was only a mile or so down the road to the home from our house. The staff at the home were great, and on a nice day, one of the carers would put her in a wheelchair, take her down to the promenade, and buy her an ice cream.

My brother Ron had a chest infection, and I took him to the doctor. Whilst I was there, I spoke about his mobile home, as I felt it was damp and was not helping his condition. The doctor sympathised when I explained that my brother could not afford to rent a flat, but said there wasn't much he could do. This only made me more determined. So many people in life who have difficulties just don't get the help they need, and there is unclaimed money they are entitled to but just don't know about.

So I wrote a few letters, and made a bit of a nuisance of myself, which I had had to do to help Phil in the past, and eventually my brother was given income support to boost his pension, and best of all, a place in local council run sheltered housing, which he could now afford. This was such a relief to me, because I knew he would now be warm and dry.

In that same year, we heard that Eileen had suffered a heart attack and died. We had been planning to visit her again, but we were too late. We travelled to Devon for her funeral a few days later, and met her son Michael, who had arranged everything. My brother Ron also came. Eileen had made him very welcome, and he had visited her for short breaks quite frequently.

At the church there were many well wishers and family, I wish she could have seen how popular she was. Her brother Don spoke about how caring she had been. Firstly she took care of her husband Alan before he died. Then a family friend from years

h

before had moved in after his wife died. His name was Ron, and he had once been a newspaper reporter. Eileen cared for him before he passed away, and she never complained about it, or said it was hard work. I will not only remember her as a good friend, but also a lady with the kindest heart and an indomitable will.

Chapter Twenty-six

In May 2012 Keith's mother Joy passed peacefully away one night. We had been expecting it since January that year. The manager of the home had warned us, but it was still a shock when we got the news. She was ninety-two years old. Keith had always looked after his mother very well, and lived near to her after his dad passed away, She had always treated me with kindness, and we both felt the loss of her.

Together with his brother, he took on the task of selling her bungalow, and dealing with all the legalities that have to be sorted out when someone dies. When we arranged the funeral, after discussion, we decided to hold the wake at our house. We had checked out some local halls and pubs, but they seemed cold and unfriendly, and we felt Joy would have liked the idea of all her relatives getting together in a family environment.

We arranged for a local supermarket to do the catering. I gave them the date, and arranged to go and pick up the food when it was ready. I spent the early part of that morning cleaning and polishing the house, and by then Keith's brother and his wife had arrived. We went to collect the food, but there wasn't any, as the supermarket claimed I had given them a different date!

I knew we had to move quickly, so we ended up buying the food there and then, and doing the catering ourselves; just about getting it ready for when it was time to go to the funeral. I was mortified at the mistake I had made, because I had so wanted everything to be perfect for Joy. But when I apologised, one of the guests remarked that Joy would have found it funny, because she had always had a great sense of humour; which made me feel so much better. It's amazing how kind people can be in times of great stress.

It was during that year I decided to write another novel. I had great fun creating Sadie Morton Brown, a woman so evil she would stop at nothing to get what she wanted in life. I have always found dark stories interesting, so I decided to create one of my own. The way she behaved begs the question, was Sadie born evil, or did something happen during her life to make her that way? Her dark deeds were shocking, and I didn't know what reaction to expect. My publisher liked the story, and accepted it to be published in 2013.

My books had been on Amazon for many years, but it occurred to me, that if I went out and met people, I might sell them even more quickly. I was planning to contact libraries, bookshops, and anywhere that I thought might be interested in stocking my new book.

But in the meantime, I had a friend called Kevin, who was also an author and had a new book coming out as well, so we teamed up together going to book fairs and sharing a table; not really knowing what to expect. What became obvious immediately, was that people were very interested in my first book about Phil titled *My Life is Worth Living!*. Autism was becoming an interesting subject, and it seemed quite a few people suffered from it in some form or another. I sold quite a few copies, as people were interested to hear about my family's experiences.

We were now going regularly to the bungalow in Suffolk. We were enjoying it so much, we had decided not to let it out, but to use it ourselves. I visited various libraries and bookshops around Suffolk and Norfolk to inform them about my fast approaching publication day, and found I had great support.

Amongst the sadness of life, there are also happy occasions, as the pendulum of time swings back and forth. In Great Britain we celebrated our Queen's sixty years on the throne, and we basked in the glory of our Olympic and Paralympic Athletes.

By the time 2013 arrived, Keith and I decided it was time we had a family cat again. We knew that Leo would get on fine with it, just as he had with Charley, so we had no worries about that. It seemed a good idea to rescue one, so we contacted our local RSPCA. We had decided it ought to be a kitten, so it could grow up knowing Leo right from the start, as we felt a fully grown cat might not be able to cope. But they didn't have any kittens at that time.

Keith had a fancy to have a ginger cat. I didn't mind, and there was a ginger kitten advertised locally, so we phoned up, and arranged to go and view it. When we got to the house, the lady explained it was three months old and very friendly. He was sitting on the floor in the kitchen, so she urged me to pick him up, which I did, but he was having none of it; he stuck his claws in me, and then ran under the table.

That was a shock to me, as I love all animals, and I usually find when I go to people's houses, their cat always wants to sit on me. Keith is like the pied piper, it's a standing joke with us, so he bent down to see if he could coax the kitten from under the table. But out came the claws again; he was not at all sociable.

The lady then fished him out and held him. He was certainly a very pretty little cat, and she seemed undeterred by the fact that he had just drawn blood from both of us. She was most surprised when we said we would go home and give it some thought, then let her know if we wanted him.

When we got outside, Keith remarked that if he was a friendly cat, he would hate to see an unfriendly one, and we had a little laugh about it.

A few days later, the RSPCA phoned up to say they had a litter of kittens: two boys and two tabby girls. I told Keith, and we arranged to go and see them. On the way there, he remarked that he didn't want a black cat because he felt they were boring.

When we saw them, they were so tiny, just six weeks old. Apparently their mother was only four months old herself, and she had been attacked. The kittens were the result, and she rejected them because she didn't know what they were. She had attacked them, so they had to be removed from her immediately.

They looked so helpless and vulnerable, and were in a child's playpen. The two females were both tabby, one boy was black and white, and the other one was all black. The lady then explained that they wanted to home them in pairs, as they were very close to each other, especially as there had been no love from their mother.

The lady advised us that the black and white boy might not be a good choice, as he had shown a bossy side to his nature, which is pretty amazing at six weeks, and he might not bond with Leo. I didn't think that Keith would want the black cat, so it looked like we would be adopting the two tabby girls.

But our little black kitten had other ideas; he headed across the playpen towards Keith, jumped onto his lap and stayed there. After playing with him for a few minutes Keith said:

"Well I am definitely having this one, which one do you want?"

I had to smile to myself. For all Keith's big words, this little kitten had charmed him into having a black cat, and since that day he has found out that black cats are not at all boring, they have very interesting characters.

I chose one of the tabby girls. She was the one who seemed closest to the black male and they rubbed noses; and have always greeted each other in that way when they come back into the house at night ever since. We were not impressed with their adopted names of Larry and Elsie, so we changed them to Max and Mia.

Leo was as gentle with them as I thought he would be, just once when she saw him did Mia hiss at him. He took no notice, and by the end of the first day, they realised he was harmless. Max particularly revered Leo. He would come in from the garden, then walk underneath him, swishing his tail so Leo knew he was there. Leo was so long suffering, and he was incredibly respectful and gentle towards them. In the morning, when it was time to go out, he always waited until they had gone through the back door into the garden, then dutifully exited behind them. It was great to see them living together and getting on so well.

So *Evil Woman* was published. I had deliberately chosen an arresting title, and my publisher had supported me by finding a cover design which was guaranteed to create interest. He also backed it up by making a matching bookmark which has obviously helped to get me more sales.

Later in 2013, we had some very happy news. Becky, my eldest granddaughter in America, was getting married to Nate. We had met him during our annual visit to America, and he was such a nice man, we knew he would make her happy. Becky was now twenty-three, and what a kind caring young lady she had grown up to be. Indeed it was the same for Katey and Ashley. It must be very hard for girls to grow up without a mother, especially when they reach their teens, but Tom has done an amazing job with them. They are all so well grounded and independent, and he has every right to feel proud of them. The feeling has never left me that it's not fair that Anita was deprived of seeing her beautiful girls blossom and become young women, but I do not allow it to fester. Just once in a while, when I see them, or speak to them, I feel the injustice of it.

The wedding was fixed for just after Christmas, which meant I had to do some shuffling around as regards to making arrangements for having Phil. At Christmas Mick and I share Phil, and it alternates each year between who has him on Christmas Day, and then the other one has him from Boxing Day onwards. But on this occasion, Mick would also be at the wedding, and we had to fly out there on 27th December.

So we had Phil earlier than usual, and he spent Christmas Day with us, then on Boxing Day we took him back to Hastings. The staff had very kindly said they would come in that day to receive him back so that we could go home and get ourselves ready to fly out the next day.

Imogen was now almost fourteen, and was keen to come with us. She had not seen her cousins since they had stayed at our cottage back in 2003, and they were obviously going to see a huge difference in her. With her long auburn hair, and a little bit of make-up, she was looking very grown up.

We flew to Washington and hired a car, which Keith drove. The traffic was horrendous, and I felt sorry for him, as after eight hours of flying, he must have felt as tired as me. It was particularly stressful because we knew they had arranged a special dinner that evening for all the family, which is tradition in America just before a wedding. It was going to be a three course meal, and as the time ticked away, it was obvious to us that we were not going to get there in time, and we could not expect them to hold it up for us.

We finally arrived, a bit hot and breathless, but it didn't seem to matter, with so many of the family getting up to greet us and make us welcome. Then they found somewhere for us to sit. We were by now very hungry, so the food was a very welcome sight.

It was a lovely meal, and we were able to catch up with all the latest family news. The girls found it hard to equate their fourteen year old cousin, who was now into make-up and lovely clothes, with the little three year old they had seen when they visited me in 2003. But it was like they had never been apart; there was immediately a rapport between them.

The day of the wedding dawned sunny and bright. It was about fifteen degrees, which considering it was winter, I thought was very warm. I had taken a chance on it not being too cold. My dress was lemon flowers on a lilac background, and I had a lilac jacket to match it. I had managed to get lilac shoes and a handbag to match, but the shoes were not made for walking, they had pointed toes with stiletto heels.

Becky had a beautiful dress, looking every inch the radiant bride, with lace detail at the top and a nipped-in waist, and her sisters, who were her bridesmaids, wore black, which did look very classy, and they carried matching handbags. They had all been to the nail bar and the hairdresser earlier in the day, and Carol also wore a very sophisticated black dress.

Seeing Becky enter the church on her dad's arm brought tears to my eyes. His girls were Tom's whole world, and he was just about to lose his eldest daughter. I mentally chided myself for being silly; he would never lose her, but we all have to let our children grow up and find their own niche in life. Nate adored her, and would take good care of her, and I was sure she would still visit her dad regularly. It was impossible to ignore my heart, which was aching so much that Anita couldn't be there to see her beautiful daughter grow into a woman, and marry the man she loved.

When we came out of the church, there wasn't really anywhere very picturesque to take the wedding photos, as the church was situated on a main road and the traffic was continually driving past. So someone suggested that we went to a garden nearby. It was a bit of a walk, and by now my feet were aching in my new uncomfortable shoes, so by the time we got there, in desperation, I had to do a Sandy Shaw and take them off. My feet would not be seen in the photographs, so it didn't really matter. I walked back to the car in my stocking feet, and then put them on again as I wanted to wear them at dinner.

Afterwards we went to a very nice hotel, and we had a sit down meal. Then came the speeches, amusing and entertaining, but then Tom said a few words, and it was almost as if he had read my mind. He said that although Anita was not here in the congregation to see Becky get married, she was here in everyone's hearts, and was watching over us. It was comforting to me to know she wasn't forgotten, she never would be, and I appreciated his little speech very much.

We stayed a few more days and Imogen had fun with her cousins, and we went on some shopping trips. It was just after Christmas, so all the sales had started. We stayed until New Year; it was the first time I had celebrated it away from England. We had a nice meal first, then a family get together, so we could all welcome in 2014 together. Spending time like this with my American family on such a happy occasion felt really special, and I went home feeling very happy.

Chapter Twenty-seven

2014 was a year when new challenges presented themselves to me. I have always loved being in retail, I think it must be in my blood. I have never forgotten the seventeen very happy years that I spent at Crest China. Many local areas regularly held craft fairs, so I booked a place at a few of them, and was pleased to find I was selling the books.

It was particularly heartening when people came up to speak to me regarding my biography about Phil. Autism is a subject that touches many families in one way or another. The higher functioning autism, known as Asperger's syndrome, can be present in many very intelligent people, and it can hinder their lives too, as they find social skills difficult and can often feel isolated and alone.

Back in the nineties, when the book was first published, and very little was known or recognised about autism, I was invited to speak to the pupils at secondary school assemblies, and this gave me my first taste of public speaking. Naturally I was very nervous, as particularly with teenagers, I wasn't sure if they would even be interested. However, one headmaster remarked that I had done well, because they had actually looked at me and listened without fidgeting, which was more than they did sometimes when they were being addressed during assembly.

This really encouraged me. So one day when I was at a fair, and a lady came up to speak to me, and asked if I did club talks, I thought, why not? Not only would it be a way of spreading the word about autism, but it would also give me an opportunity to sell more of my books.

When I arrived at the venue, my heart was thudding with apprehension; I really wasn't sure how my talk would be received. I called it INSPIRATION, and I explained that because of Phil, and his courage in the face of so many difficulties, I had been inspired to write about our experiences. I also tried to inject some humour into the talk, because I think people like to be entertained, otherwise I might find someone nodding off to sleep!

The response was reassuring. Afterwards the ladies came round my table and chatted to me, and also bought my other books, so I went home feeling I had done something right. When I told a friend about it, she said if I contacted the WI organisation in Kent, they would put me on their list and it would be a way of getting more talks. So I applied to West Kent WI organisation, and then after a while I received a letter explaining that I would need to come for an audition before I could go on the list.

So I carried on doing the odd talk here and there, explaining I had yet to pass an audition for the WI, but nobody seemed particularly worried about that, and my talks always seemed to be enthusiastically received.

I also started doing craft fairs in Suffolk and Norfolk when we visited. Most of them were at the weekend, and during the year of 2014 practically every weekend was taken up with craft fairs, either in Kent whilst at home, or in Suffolk. The people of Suffolk invited me to do talks at their local clubs as well, so I was opening new circles all the time.

It soon became clear to me that I would need to write a sequel to *Evil Woman*. Not only was that request reflected in the reviews on Amazon, but people were coming up to me at craft fairs and saying how much they enjoyed the book, and when would there be a sequel? This is very satisfying for an author, because it's not just about writing the book and getting it published, it's about knowing your readers enjoyed it and want more.

So for quite a while I gave it some thought, and I decided I didn't want to write another book that would simply repeat all the bad things Sadie had done. I decided to try a different slant. So in this book, Sadie would try to be a better person for the sake of her daughter. I would also reveal in the sequel exactly what had happened in Sadie's past to make her behave the way she did.

After I had written the sequel I submitted the novel to my publisher, and he read it and approved, then told me publication

179

would be in 2015. So I concentrated on selling my books again, and every time someone bought *Evil Woman*, I was able to tell them that the sequel would be out the following year.

There is a certain camaraderie amongst stallholders at craft fairs. Each person has produced something that they have crafted themselves, and it's unique to that person. So when I am buying either birthday or Christmas presents, instead of going to the shops, or buying online, I look at what my craft friends have to offer first. Likewise they give me their custom in return, as a signed book is going to last a lot longer than a box of chocolates, or a bottle of wine.

Most of the craft fairs are at the weekend, and this suits me, as now we are retired, Keith and I always prefer to go out during the week as nowhere is as crowded, especially restaurants and pubs. Going out and meeting people has been very useful to me. There are literally millions of books on Amazon now, with so many people finding that if they can't get their own publisher, they can self publish on this platform. I didn't want to be another nameless author, so I am continuing to work hard to become known, and to keep trying to produce the best work that I can; with a lot of help from my publisher, who always has the final say. He knows more than I do, and I am guided by him.

Chapter Twenty-eight

2015 was a very happy year for me in many ways. Firstly in February, my first great-grandchild was born. It's always an amazing thing when a new life enters the world. Becky gave birth to Mary Rose, a beautiful little strawberry blonde. The reason for this is that Becky is as blonde, as Nate is dark haired. Rosie, as she is now called, bears a certain similarity to Imogen at the same age, and the colour hair is also the same, and strikingly beautiful. Imogen opted to go blonde; girls have so much choice of hair colour when they get older.

We were able to meet Rosie on Skype, when she was nestled asleep in Becky's arms. Because I live so far away, this early contact meant everything to me. I felt included, and I knew that I would definitely make a visit that year to see her. The only contact Anita and I had was the telephone, we didn't even have mobiles then, but nowadays it feels like the world has got smaller, and it's much easier to be in contact with loved ones abroad.

I originally joined FaceBook so I could chat to my granddaughters. Then I found out what a useful tool it was for advertising. It has also been a link to people I have not seen for years, as most people are on it.

I did my usual amount of self promotion just before *Evil Woman. . . Takes Revenge* was published. My local library at Herne Bay always allows me to go and sit inside with my books displayed on a table on a Saturday, and they also kindly buy copies to stock in the library. I was also lucky enough to get a write-up in the local paper, boldly entitled: 'LOCAL AUTHOR

SETS LATEST NOVEL IN THE BAY'. I had decided to do that because I know all the local spots, and I thought it would be fun to weave them into the story.

I also tried to contact various TV programmes, BBC Radio 4, and my local radio stations in Kent; without success, but I always live in hope for the future. When I was in Suffolk at a craft fair, a lady came up to my table because she was very interested in the fact that I do club talks. I explained to her that I was also promoting my new book which was due out shortly. Then she asked me if I had contacted Lesley Dolphin on BBC Radio Suffolk, as she thought she would be interested in my story. I was surprised, as I don't actually live in the county, but she seemed so certain that I sent an email to Lesley at the show.

To my amazement I received a reply immediately, inviting me to come on the show the next day. Luckily we were staying in Suffolk for a week, so the next day found Keith and I travelling to the studio in Ipswich. In fact, even if we hadn't have been there, we would have made the journey from Kent.

Lesley was not on that day, her place was taken by Sarah, and although I was very nervous, she put me at my ease immediately. She interviewed me for forty-five minutes, playing records in between. Whilst the records were playing she told me what questions she would be asking, which gave me a chance to prepare my answers.

It turned out to be a very pleasurable experience, and afterwards the BBC gave me a podcast so my friend Debs, who is my PR, could make a YouTube video of it. I am not very technically minded, and would never be able to cope without her; she has been such an asset to me. It was my first radio interview, and I will always be grateful to them for having me on the programme, especially as I was only a visitor to the county.

I was very anxious to meet Rosie. I was following her progress on FaceBook and Skype, as Becky is very good at maintaining contact, and for that reason I do think the Internet is a boon. By the time it got to September she was seven months old, so I booked myself a plane ticket. On this occasion Keith was going to stay at home and look after the animals. Hopefully, when Rosie was older, there would be a chance for him to go as well.

I was staying with Tom, as Becky and Nate were in rented accommodation, but they were travelling especially so I could see them, and staying with Tom for about three days. Now that the girls had grown up and were working, my visit was entirely different to when they had been young girls on school holidays. We had gone swimming almost every day, visited zoos, gone bowling, and to the cinema, all the things that you do when children are on holiday, but these days it was hard to find a time when they were all around together.

Tom took me out for lunch one day, and then onto his FBI office to meet some of his associates. They were giving one of the workers a send-off because she was leaving, so we had cake and there was a very happy atmosphere.

Another day Katey was around; this was when Becky and Nate had arrived. So we took Rosie out for a walk together. She was a happy baby, and she chatted and gurgled whilst we were walking her. I could hardly believe that I had finally met my great-granddaughter, and I felt privileged to be around to share a small part of her life.

Ashley was working on that day, but then free on another day, so we headed off to the pitch and putt, which has always been a favourite of ours. It was hot and sunny, but we still played two rounds of it. The crazy golf course is set amongst a gurgling stream, and beautiful flowers line the banks of it. Over the other side are motor boats; when the girls were younger we used to ride in them.

One evening we went over to Carol's house, and it was whilst we were chatting that Ashley told us when she was a little girl she thought all grandmothers were called Carol, because both of hers were. Thinking about it, that sounded quite logical to me. Carol had cooked us a very nice piece of beef on her barbecue. It seems to be a tradition in America that in the summer people cook outside, even if they don't eat outside. We only cook outside generally if we are having a barbecue.

A day or so before I went home, we had Rosie's christening. I knew that Becky had arranged it specially for whilst I was there, so I could be a part of it, and it meant so much to me. When I saw the priest anoint her forehead with holy water, and bless her, I could feel so strongly that Anita was there too, watching over her grandchild.

All too soon it was time for me to return to England. But on the day I was due to go, my flight was not until the evening, so Ashley asked me if I wanted to come and have a swim at the open air pool where she lived. It was not very far from Tom, and she shared a large flat with two other girls. They were both away at that time, and she had previously showed me around the spacious accommodation. Ashley was still at college, but she worked as a waitress in the holidays, although this particular day was a free one for her.

She arranged to come over and pick me up in her car. With Tom also at work, I thought I would give his dog Joey a walk before I went out. I had been playing ball with him and he was quite excited. As I picked up the lead, he jumped up and caught my sunglasses, pushing them against my face. It didn't hurt much, so I didn't really worry about it, I took him for a walk, and soon after I came back, Ashley arrived to pick me up.

Ashley opted to sunbathe whilst I had a swim. I actually had the pool to myself, which was nice, and I wanted to make the most of these last few hours before I boarded the plane. I was still wearing my sunglasses, as the glare of the sun was strong.

When I came out of the water, I took my sunglasses off whilst I was drying and dressing myself. I just happened to glance in the mirror, and I couldn't believe what I saw. I had a black eye and it was also badly bloodshot, and it looked like the other eye was swelling up in sympathy. I looked like I had just done ten rounds with Amir Khan. What a time for this to happen, when I was just about to board a plane. I was bound to be regarded as a suspicious character!

I showed my face to Ashley, who looked rather horrified. What amazed me was it didn't hurt at all, and I wouldn't have thought Joey's playful lunge would have caused a black eye. When Tom arrived home to take me to the airport, he was equally startled, and he commented that he was sorry I would go back to Keith looking like that.

Sure enough I was frisked at the airport, and taken to one side whilst the contents of my suitcase were examined. I realised I would have to wear my sunglasses until my face healed up. I wasn't too keen on all the horrified glances I got, so it would hide my face a little.

Keith was surprised to see me with my sunglasses on inside the airport, so I told him why, and he jokingly said, "Who have you been upsetting?"

The next day I was doing a craft fair, and I didn't want to miss it, so I spent the whole day explaining many times how I became injured, whilst trying to keep a smile on my face. I sold quite a few books that day, so maybe my arresting look had helped me. Who knows? But I was glad when my face was back to normal. It took about ten days for the black eyes to go. I hope everyone believed my explanation because it was the truth.

Chapter Twenty-nine

In the early part of 2016, I was keen to write another book. Ever since Phil was diagnosed with autism, I have been greatly interested in the subject. Because not much was known about it when Phil was born, as a family we had to find our own way to deal with it and try to help Phil. We made many mistakes along the way, but hopefully we learned from those mistakes.

I was now doing club talks regularly, and many people came to speak to me about their own experiences with autistic relatives or friends. I also researched the subject myself, and was amazed to find that less than six years before Phil was born, doctors believed the mother was to blame; in short they were called 'refrigeration mothers'. The theory was a child recoiled away from human contact because his mother had not cuddled him and given him love. These children were thought to suffer from 'infantile schizophrenia'.

I was very angry about this, feeling it was a huge injustice to mothers. Not only did they suffer the heartache of having a child with special needs, but to be blamed for it, I thought was monstrous. Luckily progress has been made since then. Dr Bernard Rimland wrote a book in 1965 in which he explained that the condition was not psychological, it was physiological, meaning a child was simply born that way, and no blame should be attached to the mother.

I wanted to write a story which also included some of my own experiences, and I hoped if there were any women out there who felt they were to blame, it might offer them some sort of comfort.

Having written about Phil, who also had learning difficulties, I decided to write about the opposite end of the spectrum, the high functioning form of autism referred to as Asperger's Syndrome. The boy in my story is incredibly able, more able than other children in his class, but lacks social skills and appropriate behaviour, so is still picked on and teased.

His mother becomes pregnant with him at a time when unmarried mothers were frowned upon, and quite often they had to have their babies adopted. When I see a programme called 'Long Lost Families', it is quite heartbreaking to see women in their seventies and eighties reuniting with sons and daughters they gave birth to in the 1950s and 60s, but were not allowed to keep. The heartbreak they must have suffered, and all those wasted years they could not spend together, is tragic.

In my story, Laura keeps her baby and then she finds out he has a form of autism, and public opinion is very much against her. So it's about how she fights to have her son accepted as he is, rather than how society at that time expected him to be. Writing that gave me an opportunity to include traits of autism, and hopefully people reading it will understand that autistic people are not odd, it's just that their brain is wired in a different way.

Finally in 2016, two years after my application, I was invited to go for my WI audition. I was very nervous, but it was so important for me to pass this test that I did my best to hide it. I was made to feel very welcome, which helped my confidence. They didn't tell me on that day whether I had passed or not, but I was told I would receive a letter within a few weeks.

When I finally received the letter to say I had passed, I was delighted. Now I could officially say I had been approved by the WI. I was able to go on their list, and I also made myself a sign which I put on my table at craft fairs, and this sign, more than anything, has helped me to get bookings.

I find making contact with people at craft fairs is invaluable in helping me to get talk bookings. I am able to explain what my talk is about, and show my books, so they have an idea of what to expect. My talks have been very well received, which is pleasing, as autism is now a part of everyday life; many people having it in one form or another. Nowadays, if a child is diagnosed when they are young, they can get the right sort of help at school and they can blossom.

My book was published in September of that year. After much deliberation with my publisher, it was entitled *The Power of Love*. Many people have remarked how attractive the cover is. I am so lucky that my publisher takes care of that part of it, leaving me to get on and write the story. In fact, he has taken great care with the covers of all my books. They say 'Don't judge a book by its cover' but in this case the cover sets the scene.

I was planning to have a book launch at home. I do this whenever I have a new release, as I think it's nice to invite friends and family for an informal gathering at my house. Leo was standing next to me whilst I was addressing the invitations. Ever since he was a puppy, I have cleaned his teeth every day; it was recommended by the vet so he could avoid having tooth surgery in later life.

I picked up his toothbrush, and when I opened his mouth, I noticed he had a swelling on his gum. It almost looked like a wasp sting. We took him to the vet the same day, as we thought he might be in pain, and the vet explained it was a growth, but nine times out of ten they were not malignant.

This was reassuring news. He said he could give him an operation, but as a precaution they would send a sample of it to be tested. The operation took place on the same day as the book launch, and when we brought him home from the vet, he was not that sleepy. He walked out of the car OK, and when all the guests started arriving, he was in his element. He always loved people, and he went from one to another, cadging titbits whenever he could.

Seeing how well he had recovered was a huge relief, so we didn't really think much more about it. But a few days later, when I was on a long walk with him, my mobile rang; it was the vet. He explained that they had tested the sample and it was melanoma, which is a form of skin cancer, and he needed us to bring Leo in so he could see whether the cancer had spread to his bones.

This was devastating news, particularly as Leo showed no signs of being ill. He was eating normally and enjoying long walks, and seemed very happy in himself. So the vet tested him, and found to our huge relief that the cancer had not spread to his bones.

However, he did say that there was no guarantee that the cancer wouldn't come back, and if it did, it would mean another operation, and this time he would dig deeper, now he knew what he was dealing with, and get it all out.

Unfortunately, within six weeks it had returned, and another operation was necessary. Leo was now eleven years old, and we didn't like the idea that he was having operations. But on the other side of the argument was the fact that for a dog of eleven, he was very fit, still enjoyed long walks, and loved his food. The vet said his recovery from the operation was remarkable, so how could we deprive out lovely dog of whatever time he had left to live his life? We now knew that we had to take each day as it came, and watch him and make sure he was happy and comfortable. I kept pushing out of my mind the idea of losing him; he had been our faithful loyal boy since he was seven weeks old.

I had some very happy news in 2016 before the year ended. Becky contacted me to say she was pregnant again, and this time Rosie was going to have a brother. Her baby boy was due in April 2017. This would be my first great-grandson, and I was thrilled. I wondered how old he would be before I got to meet him? I could already feel the urge of wanting to visit after he was born, but I had to curb it, I could visit when the time was right.

Chapter Thirty

When Leo's mouth cancer was diagnosed in September 2016, we really hoped that it could be cured. In every other way, he was a remarkably fit dog. As already mentioned, he still enjoyed long walks, and had always had a very good appetite. The vet assured us that the cancer was not giving him any pain, and when he ate, it didn't seem to hurt him or bleed.

But I did find it very stressful. I had always cleaned his teeth every day since he was a puppy, and each time he had an operation, it took about six weeks for the familiar pink swelling to return. After the fourth operation in February 2017, the vet said it wasn't fair to do any more on him, he had to take out two teeth as well this time, and he said he didn't want to start removing part of his jaw.

We agreed fully with this. Our boy was now approaching twelve years old, and we were both concerned about how we would cope when it grew again, and how large would it get before we had to make that heartbreaking decision? Then we wondered if it would hurt him to eat, and would there be blood coming out of his mouth? We couldn't bear to think of our boy suffering in any way.

However, one day in early April, the decision was taken out of our hands. We took him away with us to Suffolk for a spring break, and as usual he enjoyed all the long country walks. One particular day we were going to go out for a few hours into Stowmarket to go swimming in the pool, so Keith took him for a walk whilst I got ready.

He had only been gone for a few minutes, so I was surprised to see him come back through the front door, and Leo was limping.

"Oh, what's happened?" I asked, concerned to see him like that.

"I don't know. We were crossing the road, Leo turned, and suddenly I heard a cracking noise, it was horrible. I brought him back because I thought he might be in pain."

Well that is the worst thing that can happen when you are on holiday, I thought, but I knew he would have to go to the vet immediately. Back home he was well known by all the vets in our local surgery, but in Suffolk neither Leo nor our cats had ever been to the vets.

We managed to find a vets practice a couple of villages away, and we took him there. It was later in the day, and by then he was really struggling to walk. It absolutely broke my heart to see him like that.

We were seen by a lady vet, and obviously because we were not regulars she didn't want to be too involved. She explained that his hip joints had gone, and he would not be able to walk unless he had an operation. It was a major operation and he might not recover from it. And apart from that, the cancer was growing again too.

She then gave us some painkillers for him, and I still remember her words:

"Leo is now coming to the end of his life. If you give him these until you get home, it will help him with the pain."

I was crying by the time we got home. Not that it was of any help to the situation, but all those months of watching the cancer continuing to return had worn me down. There was no way that we could give Leo painkillers and then carry on with our holiday as if nothing had happened. So we both came to the very difficult decision that the next day we would have to let him go.

By the end of the evening we knew it was the right decision. We had to carry him out to the garden between us when he wanted to relieve himself. He could not stand up; it was so very distressing.

When we went to bed that night, he had fallen asleep on the rug in the lounge, and our bedroom was right next to it. Usually he would get up and then lay outside our bedroom door, but I doubted that he could move himself any more. I was in turmoil, and didn't expect to be able to sleep, so many emotions were going on inside me. I wanted him to have peace, but I didn't want to lose him.

We were just settling down in bed when I heard a shuffling noise, and to my amazement, somehow he had managed to get himself out of the room and into his usual position in the hall. It was clear to me that he wanted to be close to us; maybe it gave him some sort of comfort.

The next day we got up, and I felt sick inside. I have never been a brave person, but I knew I had to face this. There was one thing left for me to do to make my boy happy. He loved his food, and one of his favourite meals was tuna, so I opened a tin, and with tears in my eyes, I watched him quiver with excitement when he smelt it.

He demolished it quickly; even after everything he still loved his food. So with heavy hearts we put him in the car and took him to the vets. Again we felt there was no connection; they didn't know Leo, they just did their job. I stood with Keith, stroking Leo's furry coat, but when the needle went in and I saw his head drop, I was overwhelmed with grief. He was gone forever.

I didn't want to go back to Kent and leave him behind, but I had no choice; I had commitments back home. So we went home and broke the news to the family. Everyone was upset; Leo had been well loved.

Two weeks later we returned to collect his ashes. We took them home with us and scattered them in Bishopstone Glen, and on the beach. Those two places were where he was walked every day. I knew I would always remember the happy times after the pain of losing him passed.

We both decided that we would not have any more dogs. It wasn't just the pain of losing them, it was that my lifestyle had changed so much. I worked every weekend, spending all day at craft fairs selling my books, and we sometimes went away if I had an event where we needed to stay overnight. We no longer had anyone in the family to take care of a dog. Andrea now had a house full of cats, Jim was at work, and Betty now lived in a local care home.

Two weeks after losing Leo, we had some very happy news, which came just at the right time. Becky had been safely delivered of a baby boy. He was named after his dad, Nate, and everyone called him Natty. Once again we were able to meet him on the Internet. As usual Becky was very good with her communication, and so we got to see videos and pictures of him, and watch him developing before our eyes. He looked like our side of the family, and his grandad Tom, with blond hair and blue eyes. I was impatient to see him in the flesh, but after discussing it with Becky, I was planning to do so in early 2018. This time Keith would come with me, and he would meet both the children. It was something for us both to look forward to.

I felt it was now time for me to focus on writing a new book. Once I get an idea in my head, then I want to develop it. I have always been fascinated by identical twins, particularly if they have different personalities. So I created Rachel, a serious, studious and hard working girl, and her twin Diana, who was slightly irresponsible, fun loving and dramatic. The story is about one of the twins having a baby, and when the infant is abducted from hospital, there are three women who could have done it, including her twin. I trace the story of each woman's predicament, and why it might have been them, and the reader will then decide for themselves who it might be. The culprit is revealed at the end of the book.

After I had written it, I submitted it to my publisher, and it was accepted for publication in 2018. Every time I have a book accepted, it is a great feeling, and one that I will never take for granted. Having spent some time creating characters and plots, to know that my work was entertaining enough to be released to the public is very heartening.

During that same year, sales of *My Life is Worth Living!* had been going very well, and it became obvious that by the end of the next year, if not before, we would have sold all the hardback copies. I spoke to my publisher about it, as that book is the basis of my talk about 'Inspiration', so I can never be without it. To my delight he informed me that he would be reprinting it in paperback, and it would also be available on Kindle, as when it was originally published in 1993, Kindles were not around.

It was my turn to have Phil on Christmas Day that year, and then Mick would have him from Boxing Day onwards. The week before Christmas, Keith was in Suffolk; I couldn't go because I had Christmas fairs to go to, and also the house to organise and get ready before my family arrived.

j

I really wasn't feeling well that week. My chest was tight, and I thought trust me to get a cold at my busiest time of the year. After a few days I took to my bed. I couldn't stand up properly, so I thought it must be flu. However, I was determined to beat it; nothing would stop me from spending Christmas with those whom I love the most. But as the days passed, I wasn't feeling any better and I had a pain on the left side of my chest, so I couldn't settle comfortably in bed.

Keith arrived home on the day before Christmas Eve and was amazed to find me in bed. He knew that if I was in bed I must feel ill, as it was so unusual. Until then I hadn't visited a doctor for years, I simply went to the surgery to get my annual flu jab.

The next morning, which was Christmas Eve, I still couldn't get out of bed. I wanted to sleep, but my pain made it impossible for me to get comfortable. I told Keith I would be OK if I just had some sleep. He told me afterwards that my colour was grey, so he telephoned 111 services, but they were not operating because it was Christmas. So then he phoned 999, and described my symptoms. It probably sounded worse than it was with chest pains, but within minutes an ambulance arrived with two paramedics. They explained that they had been diverted from another call to come and see me, although at the time I didn't absorb that.

They gave me various tests and assessed my condition. They then said that the poison had gone into my bloodstream and they would need to get me to hospital immediately. I was blissfully unaware it was serious, but Keith had realised by now that it was. All I felt was heartbroken that I was being taken away from my family at such a time.

When we arrived at the hospital I was taken immediately to Casualty. As they wheeled me through, and I saw all the people waiting, I thought we were in for a long wait; but no, I was wheeled straight into the doctor, and at that moment I realised that I might be seriously ill.

It turned out that I had pneumonia, and I was treated intravenously with drugs injected straight into my bloodstream. I was also attached to a glucose drip. The reason for the haste was that it had affected the left side of my lung, but fortunately it was caught in time, and did not progress to being double pneumonia. Antibiotics alone would not have stopped it spreading, but being treated straight into my veins halted the progress. I feel I must mention the two paramedics who came to my aid. They were so kind and efficient, and got me so quickly to hospital, otherwise my illness would have been a lot more serious. I am truly grateful, I could not have had better service, so well done to them; and also well done to the doctors and nurses at the QEQM hospital at Margate. I also feel I must mention what a great job Keith did in my absence. For the first time ever, he cooked Christmas dinner for Jim, Phil, Ron and himself, and gave them lashings of mashed potato, which he cooked and mashed himself. He couldn't find the Christmas pudding, but they all enjoyed fruit cocktail and double cream.

Andrea and David came, as did Keith, Ron and Jim, to visit me in hospital on Christmas Day, so I did see them, but not in the way I had imagined. Even my granddaughter Imogen came, and I reassured them I would soon be as good as new, and declared that 2018 was going to be a very busy year for me with two books coming out.

I remained in hospital for five days, and every day I felt stronger. The medication was working, and I started to eat again. The hospital staff were kind and caring, and I have nothing but praise for the work they do. Even though we all know how stretched and short staffed the NHS is, I was given the best possible care, which in turn helped me to make a speedy recovery. Not enough credit is given to our National Health Service; we only hear on the news about things that have gone wrong. However, we had to make use of it for years when Phil was in and out of hospital, and now I had needed urgent and efficient treatment to get me well quickly, and they delivered. Well done to everyone concerned!

Chapter Thirty-one

I had to return to the hospital for an outpatient's appointment in early January 2018. The doctor was happy with my progress, but did say that I would feel quite weak for a while, and it would take me about six weeks to three months to get back to normal.

This put me in a quandary, as I was already feeling pretty good, and we had planned to go and visit the family in America. My free month was February, as after that my craft fairs and talks started. Rosie's third birthday was in February, and I really wanted to be a part of it. But I had lost a bit of confidence after being ill and I didn't want to overdo it, and make my recovery take longer.

By the time we got to early February I was feeling fine, so I took a chance and we booked our tickets; after all, life is for living!

Becky and Nate had recently bought their own house, and now lived in Charlotte, which was also conveniently near to the airport, and they had plenty of room for us to stay. A week or so before we were due to fly out, Becky messaged me on FaceBook; she was very excited. Even though it was only mid February, the weather forecast for the period we were coming was warm, about seventy degrees, which is highly unusual so early in the year. This had made her decide that they would take us to the coast for a couple of days, so we were booked into a very nice hotel right next to the beach.

When we arrived I was expecting Rosie and Natty to be very shy. Rosie would not remember me from 2015, and Natty was ten months old. But not so, they rushed out of the front door to greet us, and I felt a wave of pride inside me when I saw what happy friendly children they were. I felt so proud to be a great-grandmother, and still be agile enough to play with them and have fun. By the time the evening came they were cuddling us, and it was like we had known them forever.

We had the most amazing holiday with them, and I am sure it hastened my recovery. The sun shone, and we had a great time at the beach. It wasn't warm enough to go in the water, but we played with the children and built sandcastles. Rosie took her bucket down to the sea to fill it with water so she could fill up the moat that had been made for her. The hotel was excellent, and when we got up in the morning, we went to a local place to get our breakfast.

It was at the beach we met up with Tom, who is such a proud granddad, and rightly so. Natty bears a strong resemblance to him. Anita and Tom both had blonde hair and blue eyes, and could be taken for brother and sister, so Natty resembles both sides of his grandparents' families.

We packed so much into our visit there. Walks with the children, outings to the shops, and then at the weekend Becky had a birthday party for Rosie, and that was our time to get together with the family, as Ashley, Carol, and Nate's parents Pam and Davood, as well as Tom came. Sadly I didn't get to see Katey as she lives in California and could not get the time off work. I did speak to her on the telephone, but it's never the same.

All too soon it was time to return to England, and with the sadness always inside me that I can only have a brief glimpse into their lives, we left our family and flew home. We had made some wonderful memories to treasure.

My new book *One Moment of Madness* was published in April. Once again I held a book launch at home for friends and family to come. I don't hold it in a hall because it's more of a party, with food and home-made punch, and an opportunity for everyone to catch up with each other. I sold quite a few copies of the new book, which always helps to give it a start.

When we lost Leo the year before, although it was heartbreaking, memories come back to you afterwards of all the good times we spent together. I missed him getting up on the sofa for a cuddle in the evening, and taking up much of it, bless him. I also missed the welcome he always gave us when we came in. The most wonderful thing about a dog is that they don't judge us, they accept us for who we are, so if we come home in a bad mood, the joyous reception you get from your dog is very soothing. I missed his little face at the door, and his wagging tail. I missed the feeling of being safe he gave me when we were on our own. He had a bark like an alsatian, but if truth was known, if a burglar had come in, he probably would have licked them to death. I missed all our lovely walks on the beach, and out in the countryside. And all my fine words about never having another dog just melted away, and I knew I wanted that companionship again.

But Keith, ever sensible, pointed out that our lifestyle now made it hard to have a dog. We were out a lot, especially me, and he thought it wasn't fair on the cats, because another dog might not be as respectful and gentle with them as Leo had been, and we couldn't take a dog out in the car and leave it at any time, that was unthinkable!

I knew what he was saying was right, but I still couldn't get rid of that ache in my heart; Leo had left such a void in my life. Going for walks without him just didn't mean the same any more, and so I decided that I would find someone who could have our dog all day if we were out, and also a dog walker. I could and would make it work because it was that important to me.

I explained all this to Keith, and he reluctantly agreed that we could look around. I knew he wasn't keen, and I expect I was being selfish, but I said I would be the dog's primary carer and walker. If he wanted to go out when I was also out, I would pay for its care.

First of all we tried our local Dogs Trust, because it's nice to know you can give a dog a better life than they had before. We wanted a collie type dog; not too big. Living where we are with fields and beaches, it's ideal for an active dog. Keith and I are still very young at heart, and we love long walks. We wanted a fun dog, who would like playing ball, and maybe even swimming in the sea.

We were hoping to get a puppy, or a dog at least no older than a year, so we could train it not to chase the cats. Well, that is what we hoped for. But there are loads of other people also wanting a young dog, and although we went up there every time a new arrival came that might be suitable, there were always about three or four other people wanting the same dog.

It was quite amusing one day when a one year old collie type dog was advertised on their website. He looked gorgeous, and in a bid to stand any sort of chance, we arrived at the Dogs Home half an hour before it opened. There was a couple in front we started talking to, and I realised to my horror that they were after the same dog. I shouldn't have mentioned that we were after a collie type, because as soon as the gate opened, the lady, who was probably about fifty, sprinted up the drive so she could get there before us.

But it doesn't work that way with dog rescue; it's not first come first served, it's who is most suited to that dog. Several of us were interviewed, and then we got to see him. He was a lovely boy, but I wasn't sure how he would be with Max and Mia, and after all they were here first. I also felt very sorry for this desperate lady, because evidently they had driven all the way from Sussex, so we said we would keep looking and went home.

It was whilst we were in Suffolk that I saw an advertisement with Pets at Home on the Internet. A collie/spaniel cross breed was advertised for sale in Norfolk. He was the last of a litter of ten, and three months old. I emailed the owner and asked the usual questions: "Has he been 'defleaed' and wormed? Can I see his mother?" The answers came back.

"Yes, he's ready to go, and his mother can be seen; she is our family pet."

Keith was still not too happy, so I knew I would have to get this done and dusted before he had a chance to worry about it. I knew because of his love for all animals, once we got the dog, he would be fine.

But fate wasn't really much on my side. We were given an address, which according to our satnav when we got there, didn't exist. We were sitting in the car and I was wondering what to do, whilst Keith was grumbling about what a waste of time it had been, when suddenly my mobile sprang into action.

A female voice enquired if I was Carol, and I said I was. She then said her partner would come and meet me at the end of the road and guide us to where they lived, as it was difficult to find.

As it was near to countryside, I had visions of a little cottage set back from the road.

A young man with a very cheerful face greeted us at the end of the road, and we offered him a lift in the car, which he declined, saying he would walk ahead and show us the way.

We drove past the local police station, and then there was a turning which he took, and we followed in the car. I have never been more gobsmacked at the scene that met our eyes. It was a concrete car park with a gypsy caravan parked there. Outside running around on rope, and sounding very aggressive, were five or six dogs, including a collie. They were leaping towards us barking loudly, and he yelled at them to shut up.

I didn't look at Keith, because I knew he would not want to get involved, and I heard him say, "I think we need to turn this car right round and head off."

But I had come so far, not just in miles, but emotionally, so at that moment I chose to have selective hearing, and I opened the car door and sprang out. The caravan door opened and a young woman holding a little girl in her arms invited us in to see the puppy.

Poor Keith didn't really have much choice other than to follow me. I wonder why he puts up with me? The inside of the caravan left much to be desired, but there on the floor was a puppy, all black except a white flash on his chest and three of his paws.

Once I picked him up and he was in my arms, I knew I had to take him home with me. I am not suggesting they were cruel to him, in fact the young man has contacted me by text since then and asked for a photo of him to see how he is doing. But I knew we could give him such a great life. He is a very active dog, and would not have coped with being tied up.

He nestled into my lap, and it felt right again. The love of a dog is very special, and here we had a tiny puppy who would be dependant on us to give him a good life. We asked the question about cats, explaining we had two, but the young man told us that he had never even seen a cat.

I didn't dare look at Keith. I knew that there would be doubt written all over his face, but nothing was going to stop me now. So I paid the man, and hugging the little one to me, went and got in the car. When I had asked if he was house trained, although he said "Sort of," I wasn't convinced, so I laid a towel over my lap in case of any accidents.

For most of my life I have fallen in with what other people want, because I like everyone to be happy, but the longing inside me to have another dog was so strong, I just couldn't ignore it. The drive back to our bungalow was over an hour, and he was so good in my arms. We decided in the car to call him Ben, and I felt by the time we got back, Keith's manner towards him was softening.

That night he slept on the floor next to the bed. He didn't move from there, and in the morning I took him out in the garden and he obliged me with a wee. But by now his shyness from first meeting us vanished. Ben became a one dog destruction team. He chewed slippers, ripped up tissues, destroyed all our coasters, ran off with socks and knickers, anything to make us chase him; we had a fun dog all right, but he was the only one laughing!

We were not impressed when he chased the cats; we repeatedly told him not to. We got used to putting our hot mugs on half eaten coasters. We hid all our shoes where he couldn't reach them; he wasn't going to outsmart us, but then he ran off with the plastic dishes that the cats use, and they had chew marks all over them. I had to buy him a stone feeding bowl; let him try running off with that!

He couldn't be left alone in a room because he was so destructive, so we bought him a crate. We never used one for our other dogs, but Ben is Ben, and luckily for us he loves it and never complains when he goes in it.

Keith remarked that he should be a mascot for the programme 'Destroyed in Seconds'. But having told you all the bad stuff, these are his good points.

He is the most loving dog you can find, he makes friends with everyone, and he doesn't have an aggressive bone in his body. He is very intelligent, he walks nicely on the lead, and he eats well. He has such charm; after being with him for just a few minutes, everyone is captivated, including us, and you have to forgive him anything.

He must have got the vibes that Keith was the reluctant owner, because after a short time he attached himself to him. He cuddled up to him at night on the sofa, followed him around the house, and whimpered when he went out if he didn't take him with him. We both adore him, and are looking forward to the time when he doesn't destroy everything; he has to grow up eventually.

Most autistic people like dogs, but Phil is the exception, he has never taken much notice of any of our dogs. They have always sat respectfully near to his feet, but never invading his space. But Ben made up his mind that Phil would notice him, and right from the start, his evening ritual after Phil had a bath and was in his dressing gown, was to jump up next to him on the sofa, and then lay next to him upside down with his legs in the air. In the beginning Phil pushed him away and looked annoyed, but Ben was having none of it. When he gets up now Phil smiles at him; he never gave up trying to win him over, and he has succeeded.

On 19th May 2018 Prince Harry married Meghan Markle, an American actress of mixed race. Britain embraced her and it made the ties between Britain and America even stronger. After losing his mother at such a young age, I was delighted to see Harry marry the woman he loves, and I am sure his mother is looking down on them and blessing their union.

Chapter Thirty-two

During the summer of 2018 I met a lovely lady called Janis, who had a gift shop in a parade of shops in Beltinge, which is a small village. She invited me to come and do my 'Inspiration' talk at her shop. The shop was called The Green Room, and it had a variety of very tempting items inside.

When I arrived at the shop there were several people gathered, and Janis, always the perfect hostess, served tea, coffee and home made cake to them all. My talk was very well received, and afterwards I had a lot of support. They were interested in all my books, and I made a lot of sales.

Because she could only get a limited amount of people in her shop at one time, Janis invited me back on two more occasions to different circles, and I did my talk and sold my books again. Afterwards she invited me to have a shelf in her shop for my books and it proved to be a big success, and on my behalf, in the shop, she made a lot of sales to local villagers.

Janis worked very hard to make her business a success. The shop was always beautifully set out, and the window had many interesting and attractive things in it. I bought several items from her, and have been delighted with them, especially the oak clock which I have situated just above an oak display cabinet in our conservatory.

Sadly her shop closed at Christmas, and has now become an estate agency. Janis is a remarkable lady, as she took care of her father until he died, and is now a full time carer to her mother. I truly miss popping in to see Janis and sharing a coffee with her. I want to thank her for all the support she gave me, and all the sales she made for me when I wasn't in the shop. Thanks to Janis, my sales that year were the highest they had ever been.

I started the early part of 2019 with a week's holiday in Malta with Keith and his brother Brian and Jackie. Unfortunately we chose the wrong week. There were storms and snow, which is so rare in Malta. It was meant to be a few days of winter sunshine before all my events started, but I should have stayed in Herne Bay, as during that week, the temperatures rose to an unbelievable twenty degrees, which is very rare in February.

By the end of 2018, to my delight, we had sold all the hardback copies of *My Life is Worth Living!* My publisher was as good as his word. On 22nd February 2019, which also happens to be a family birthday, the paperback version was released for publication, and a kindle version was also made available. The new book is now selling steadily. I believe there are a few second-hand copies of the old one available on Amazon for not much more than the cost of postage. Writing that book for me was a means of sharing our story with other families who may be similarly affected, and I do hope it offers some sort of comfort and hope to mothers who may feel very alone; I did at the time, even with a loving family around me.

I started up again doing craft fairs and book signings, as well as talks in March, and at one of the craft fairs, I was approached by Emma, an artist. She explained that she was setting up a shop in Canterbury and it was going to house over one hundred different artisans, all of whom created their own work, and she said how much she would like to have my books in there.

I have always wanted to get my books into a shop, and Canterbury is a very busy thriving city, so I gratefully accepted. As I write this, in June 2019, she has set up a special book signing event for me on 23rd June. The shop is called 'Walrus and Oyster Emporium', and Emma has worked very hard in setting it up. There are so many diverse crafts, all lovingly made. When people come in to browse their reaction is very encouraging, and good sales have been made.

Back at home, Ben is now one year old, and we are finally seeing him integrate with our cats, and they no longer seem scared of him. They are now all in one room, but we have to remind him not to overwhelm them, or smother them with kisses.

He has grown into an amazing family dog. He is loving, affectionate, enjoys very long walks, and loves swimming in the sea. He is still naughty at times, but when he sidles up to you, and fixes his big brown eyes on you, then snuggles up to you, all is forgiven.

Now our house feels like a home again; even Keith is glad that we got him, and he adores Keith. There was no way that he was going to let Keith disapprove of him. He's a very clever dog, and he knew who he had to win over. I loved him from the moment I saw him. He loves everyone he meets, there isn't a mean bone in his body, and now I feel complete with a dog in the house.

I found a local lady who can have him if I have an event that takes me away for the day, and also a dog walker who helps out from time to time. Ben loves them all. He is such a happy dog, and the welcome he gives us when we come home can only be described as very exuberant. By the way, we tried to feed him up because we thought he was too thin, but have now realised because he runs so fast, that he is in fact a collie/whippet cross, and is meant to be thin. It doesn't matter to us what breed he is; he is our lovely boy.

I still go to my badminton club. We also play tennis and go swimming regularly, and of course go for long walks. I hope to continue writing; my mind is always full of ideas, and I enjoy creating my own little world of characters and plots.

I have a lot of friends on FaceBook who are Lewis Hamilton fans, and we often exchange gossip and photos. I had asked Keith if we could go to the British Grand Prix, just once, as I am not getting any younger, and I wanted to soak up the atmosphere and join in the support for our British Champion.

Keith has been a Formula One fan since the 70s, and also been to races, but has no desire to do so any more. He doesn't like the crowds, or queuing for the toilets, and there is a host of other reasons why he doesn't want to go. So I resigned myself to watching it on TV instead.

But I had reckoned without Jo and Helena. Jo told me that she has a tent that sleeps ten, and she had two spaces left. She was taking one person from the south of England, and one from the north. She invited me to be the person from the south. As far as I am concerned, it's a dream come true. I am finally going to go, and Helena is driving me there. I just have to drive myself to her house. I cannot believe how lucky I am, and what great friends I have.

Before I finish my story, there are so many people I would like to mention. They have all had an impact on my life. My parents for bringing me into the world, and setting a proper example to me in life. My dear brother; I am always here if you need me. My dearest John; I think of you every day. My beautiful Anita, taken far too soon, and baby Emily. Jim and Andrea, for all your love, loyalty and support. Dear Phil, for just being Phil; I love you. For Keith, a true friend and partner. Then of course my family in America: Carol and Tom, Becky and Nate, and little Rosie and Natty. Katey and Ashley, and dear Joey the dog.

For Malcolm and Valerie, thank you for my *Evil Woman* website, and Debs, thank you for all the videos and my YouTube Channel, and everything else you have done for me. I could never have managed without you! For Lesley and John, Mo, Ann and Peter, and Carole and Nick, thanks for lifting me up when I felt low. One particular occasion sticks in my mind. It was one of my sad anniversaries, and I was feeling a bit low, and I admitted it. A few days later I was at a craft fair, and who should walk in the door to see me but Lesley and Jon with some flowers. That visit, and knowing how much you cared, was everything to me. God bless you both! Thank you to Dawn and Maria for helping in selling my books, and to all my friends, every one of you mean so much to me, and I hope I never take any of you for granted. For all my new friends and readers on FaceBook, such as Megan, Haydn, Lucie, Pearl and many more, I cannot mention you all, but I am so very grateful for your support!

My life has been full of ups and downs just like everyone else. I have had many happy times, and a few sad times too. Losing those so dear to me was a learning curve. I never got over it, I just learned to rebuild my life. But I still feel them in my heart, close to me, and that gives me comfort.

Thank you everyone for letting me share my story with you, God bless you all!